A Country Store In Your Mailbox®

Merry Christmas!

A Country Store In Your Mailbox®

Gooseberry Patch
600 London Road
Department Book
Delaware, OH 43015
★
1·800·854·6673
www.gooseberrypatch.com

Copyright 2003, Gooseberry Patch 1-931890-22-6
First Printing, April, 2003

How To Subscribe

Would you like to receive
"A Country Store in Your Mailbox"®?
For a 2-year subscription to our
Gooseberry Patch catalog, simply send $3.00 to:

Gooseberry Patch ★ P.O. Box 190 ★ 600 London Road ★ Delaware, Ohio 43015

Contents

Dedication

For our friends & family...may your
holidays be filled with love and joy.

Appreciation

Thanks to all who shared their
family recipes and sweet
holiday memories...you make
every day merry!

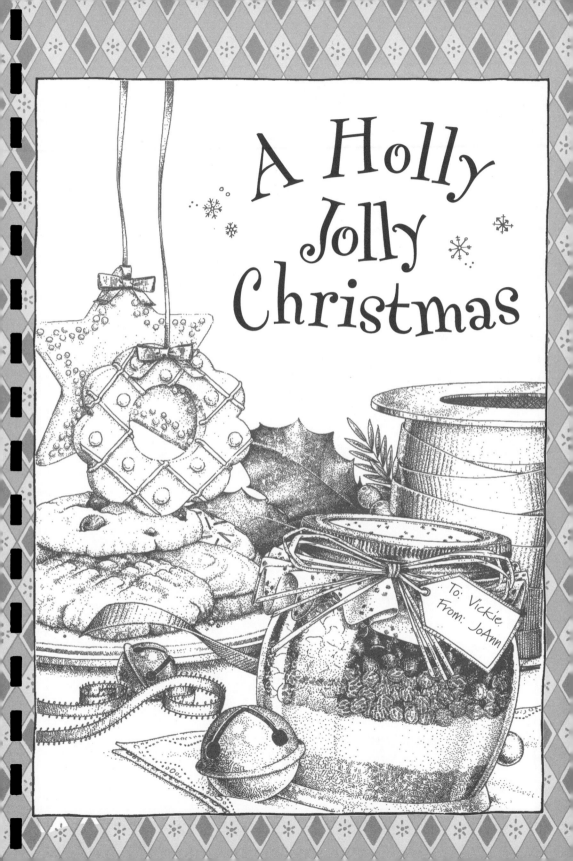

A Holly Jolly Christmas

To: Vickie
From: JoAnn

Old-Fashioned Butterscotch Candy

Melissa Bromen
Marshall, MN

I cherish the time I spent in the kitchen with my mom when I was a teenager, and I think of her every time I make this.

2 c. brown sugar, packed
3/4 c. water

1/4 c. butter
1/8 t. salt

Combine all ingredients in a saucepan. Cook over low heat, stirring until sugar dissolves. Continue cooking, without stirring, until mixture reaches the hard-crack stage, or 290 to 310 degrees on a candy thermometer. Pour into a buttered 8"x8" baking pan. Cool slightly; score into squares. When cooled, break into pieces. Makes 3/4 pound.

Chewy Peanut Logs

Janet Atherton
Algona, IA

A homemade treat to add to any gift box.

1 t. vanilla extract
1/2 t. almond extract
7-oz. jar marshmallow creme
3-1/2 to 4 c. powdered sugar

1-1/2 lbs. caramels, unwrapped
2 T. water
6 c. salted peanuts

Mix together first 3 ingredients; add powdered sugar, kneading well. Form mixture into 6 small logs. Combine caramels and water in a double boiler; heat over medium-low until melted. Dip each log in caramel; roll in peanuts. Wrap each log in plastic wrap and chill. Makes 6 logs.

Take-out containers are ideal for filling with homemade treats...just tie with a colorful ribbon and it's ready in a jiffy!

A Holly Jolly Christmas

Cranberry-Chip Cookie Mix
Lynne Takayesu-Wulfestieg
Downely, CA

A new spin...substitute dried strawberries!

1-1/8 c. all-purpose flour	1/3 c. brown sugar, packed
1/2 c. quick-cooking oats, uncooked	1/3 c. sugar
	1/2 c. dried cranberries
1/2 t. baking soda	1/2 c. white chocolate chips
1/2 t. salt	1/2 c. chopped walnuts

Layer all ingredients, in order, in a one-quart, wide-mouth jar; pack down tightly after each addition. Secure lid and tie on baking instructions.

Instructions:

Cream together 1/2 cup softened butter, one egg and one teaspoon vanilla extract in a medium bowl. Add jar contents; mix until well blended. Drop by rounded teaspoonfuls onto greased baking sheets. Bake at 350 degrees for 8 to 10 minutes or until the edges turn golden. Cool on wire racks. Makes about 3 dozen.

For a thoughtful hostess gift, dress up the lid on a jar of Cranberry-Chip Cookie Mix with greenery and berries, then tie on a festive ribbon and a handmade gift tag...so pretty!

Cranberry-Chip Cookies

Dreamy Fudge

Peg Baker
La Rue, OH

This orange-vanilla fudge brings back happy memories
of a time gone by.

3 c. sugar
3/4 c. butter
2/3 c. whipping cream
7-oz. jar marshmallow creme
12-oz. pkg. white chocolate
    chips

3 t. orange flavoring
12 drops yellow food coloring
9 drops red food coloring

Combine sugar, butter and cream in a heavy saucepan; boil until mixture reaches the soft-ball stage, or 234 to 243 degrees on a candy thermometer. Add marshmallow creme and chips; mix well. Remove one cup mixture and set aside. Add orange flavoring and food coloring to mixture in saucepan; stir well. Pour into a greased 13"x9" baking pan. Pour reserved mixture on top and swirl with a knife. Chill and cut into squares. Makes about 3 pounds.

A holiday gift bag is just the right size for filling with treats to share with friends. Make each bag special by adding a gift-card pocket to the front. Just glue on a square of wrapping paper, leaving the top side open, and slip your gift tag inside!

Old-Fashioned Christmas Taffy

Regina Kostyu
Gooseberry Patch

In the late 1950's and early 1960's I remember always having lots of laughs and tired arms when my grandmother and aunt came for our annual Christmas taffy pull. However, my sister has another memory…the year she didn't take off her fingernail polish and it ended up in the taffy so we had to throw it out!

- 2 c. sugar
- 1 c. corn syrup
- 3 T. vinegar

- 2 T. butter
- 1 t. vanilla extract
- Optional: food coloring

Combine sugar, corn syrup and vinegar in a large saucepan over medium heat. Without stirring, heat to the hard-ball stage, or 250 to 269 degrees on a candy thermometer. Remove from heat and stir in butter, vanilla and food coloring, if desired. Pour mixture onto a buttered platter and allow to cool enough to handle. Pull taffy from one hand to another until it turns white and doesn't stick to hands. Stretch out in a long strand, 1/2-inch thick; using buttered scissors, cut into one-inch pieces. Wrap each in wax paper. Makes 3 to 4 dozen pieces.

Individually wrapped taffy squares will be a welcome sweet treat when tucked into a pair of woolly mittens!

Gingerbread Pancake Mix

Rosemary Johnson
Irondale, AL

Pair this with Homemade Maple Syrup for a Christmas morning gift!

1 c. all-purpose flour
1-1/2 t. baking powder

1/2 t. cinnamon
1/2 t. ground cloves

Mix together all ingredients; place in a plastic zipping bag. Attach instructions before giving.

Instructions:

Place mix in a medium bowl; add 3 tablespoons molasses, 1/2 cup milk, one tablespoon oil and one slightly beaten egg. Mix well. Drop batter by 1/4 cupfuls onto a hot non-stick griddle or skillet. Turn when bubbles form on the surface; heat until both sides are golden. Makes 9 pancakes.

Homemade Maple Syrup

Jana Warnell
Kalispell, MT

I always keep a batch in my fridge...it's yummy!

4 c. sugar
2 T. corn syrup
1/2 c. brown sugar, packed

2 c. water
1 t. vanilla extract
1 t. maple flavoring

Stir together first 4 ingredients in a saucepan until sugar dissolves. Heat over medium heat until boiling; boil one to 2 minutes. Remove from heat and cool 5 to 10 minutes. Stir in vanilla and maple flavoring. Makes about 4 cups.

A Holly Jolly Christmas

Ho-Ho-Hot Chocolate Mix

Donna West
Spring Creek, NV

Just a touch of cinnamon makes this cocoa delicious.

3/4 c. baking cocoa
2 c. powdered non-dairy
   creamer
1 c. sugar

2 c. powdered sugar
6 c. powdered milk
2 t. cinnamon
6 1-pint jars and lids

Mix together all ingredients; divide equally into jars. Attach gift tags with instructions onto each. Makes 6 jars.

Instructions:

Combine 1/4 cup mix with one cup hot water. Makes one serving.

Marshmallow Pops

Denise Greenberg
Little Egg Harbor, NJ

Kids will love to help make these!

10-oz. bag marshmallows
2 to 3 doz. lollipop sticks

14-oz. pkg. white melting
   chocolate, melted
colorful sprinkles

Place one to 2 marshmallows on each lollipop stick; dip each into melted chocolate to coat marshmallows. Swirl off excess and decorate with sprinkles; place on wax paper to cool. Wrap each in plastic wrap before giving. Makes 2 to 3 dozen.

Color copy nostalgic Christmas postcards...they make such pretty gift tags and jar labels.

Brown Sugar Brownie Mix

Kathy Grashoff
Fort Wayne, IN

Three ingredients make this a snap to mix up for quick gifts!

16-oz. pkg. brown sugar   1/2 c. chopped pecans
2 c. all-purpose flour

Combine all ingredients; place in a large plastic zipping bag. Attach a gift tag with baking instructions.

Instructions:

Combine Brown Sugar Brownie Mix with 4 eggs, stirring until blended. Spoon into a greased 13"x9" baking pan. Bake at 350 degrees for 25 to 28 minutes. Cool and cut into squares. Makes 3 to 4 dozen.

Place a bag of Brown Sugar Brownie Mix in the center of a festive, fabric napkin. Bring the corners up to the center and secure with a colorful napkin ring...giftwrap couldn't be easier!

A Holly Jolly Christmas

Oatmeal-Chip Cookies in a Jar

Margaret Hurayt
Millersburg, OH

It's easy to make this mix everyone's favorite cookie mix...try using butterscotch, cinnamon or mint-chocolate chips.

1 c. all-purpose flour
1/2 c. brown sugar, packed
1/2 c. sugar
1/2 t. baking soda
1/2 t. baking powder

1/2 t. salt
1 t. cinnamon
1-1/4 c. quick-cooking oats,
    uncooked
1 c. chocolate chips

Layer flour, brown sugar and sugar in a one-quart, wide-mouth jar, packing down tightly after each addition. Combine baking soda, baking powder, salt and cinnamon in a small bowl; add to jar. Place oats in jar; fill remainder of jar with chocolate chips and secure lid. Attach a gift tag with instructions.

Instructions:

Pour jar contents into a large bowl; mix in 1/2 cup oil, one egg and one teaspoon vanilla extract. Form dough into one-inch balls and arrange on ungreased baking sheets. Bake at 350 degrees for 10 to 15 minutes. Makes 3 dozen.

Bend sparkly pipe cleaners around gift tags and then glue in place...oh-so pretty and a snap to make!

Chocolatey Bon-Bons

Kristie Rigo
Friedens, PA

These are the most delicious candies I've ever made!

2 c. graham cracker crumbs
4 c. powdered sugar
1 c. flaked coconut
1 c. butter, softened
1 t. vanilla extract

1 c. crunchy peanut butter
2 T. shortening
12-oz. pkg. semi-sweet
   chocolate chips, melted

Mix graham cracker crumbs, powdered sugar and flaked coconut together; add butter, vanilla and peanut butter, mixing until combined. Roll mixture into one-inch balls. Melt shortening in a saucepan over low heat; add melted chocolate chips and stir until smooth. Dip balls in chocolate mixture and set on wax paper until set. Makes 3-1/2 dozen.

Vintage sugar sacks are just the right size for filling with gifts from the kitchen or wrapping up layered mixes. Tie a pretty ribbon around the top to keep the goodies inside a secret!

⭐ A Holly Jolly Christmas

Marshmallow Fudge

Marion Pfeifer
Smurna, DE

Creamy and oh-so rich.

1-2/3 c. sugar
2 T. butter
1/2 t. salt
2/3 c. evaporated milk
1-1/2 c. semi-sweet chocolate
    chips

2-1/2 c. mini marshmallows
3/4 c. chopped pecans
1-1/4 t. vanilla extract

Combine sugar, butter, salt and evaporated milk in a saucepan; cook over medium heat until boiling, stirring constantly. Reduce heat to low and cook at a slow boil for 8 minutes without stirring; remove from heat. Add chocolate chips, marshmallows, pecans and vanilla; stir until marshmallows are melted. Pour mixture into a greased 9"x9" baking pan. Cool and cut into squares. Makes about 1-1/2 pounds.

Cookies & Cream Truffles

Sheila Gwaltney
Johnson City, TN

These have become a staple at our house every holiday.

8-oz. pkg. cream cheese,
    softened
4 c. chocolate sandwich cookies,
    crushed

2 c. white chocolate chips
1 T. shortening

Beat cream cheese with a mixer until fluffy; blend in crushed cookies. Refrigerate for 2 hours. Roll dough into one-inch balls. Melt white chocolate chips with shortening in a double boiler over medium heat. Dip balls into mixture to coat. Place on wax paper to set; store in refrigerator. Makes 2-1/2 dozen.

Rudolph's Popcorn Balls

Lacy Mayfield
Earth, TX

My mother made these every year when I was in elementary school. My sisters and I loved to help…there's nothing like buttering your hands, forming popcorn balls and licking your fingers when you're done! My kids do the same thing in my kitchen today.

12 to 14 qts. popped popcorn
1/2 c. butter

16-oz. bag mini marshmallows
red food coloring

Place popcorn in a large roaster pan; set aside. Melt butter and marshmallows in a large saucepan over medium heat, stirring constantly. Remove from heat and stir in red food coloring to desired shade. Pour mixture over popcorn; stir well. Coat hands with butter and shape mixture into softball-size balls. Wrap each in plastic wrap. Makes 4 to 5 dozen.

Cranberry Poppers

Marj Miller
Tyler, TX

The sweet-tart flavor is a favorite of friends & family.

16-oz. pkg. cranberries

14-oz. pkg. white melting
chocolate, melted

Wash and rinse cranberries; pat dry. Dip each cranberry into melted chocolate and place on wax paper to dry. Refrigerate when set. Makes about 1-1/2 pounds.

✹ A Holly Jolly Christmas

Christmas Wreath Cookies

Kathy McLaren
Visalia, CA

Almost too pretty to eat!

1-3/4 c. all-purpose flour
1-1/2 t. baking powder
1/2 t. salt
1/2 c. shortening
1 c. sugar
1 egg
3/4 t. vanilla extract

1/4 t. almond extract
1/4 c. chopped blanched
   almonds
1 egg white, beaten
green decorating sugar
red cinnamon candies

Sift together flour, baking powder and salt; set aside. In a separate bowl, cream shortening; gradually add sugar, beating until fluffy. Blend in egg, vanilla and almond extract. Fold in almonds. Stir in dry ingredients; chill mixture for 3 hours. Divide dough in half and roll out each half between 2 sheets of wax paper to 1/8-inch thickness. Cut out cookies with a leaf-shape cutter. Arrange leaves in groups of 2 or 3 on an ungreased baking sheet; brush surfaces with egg white. Sprinkle green sugar over top of cookies and place 3 to 4 cinnamon candies at the base of the leaves. Bake at 375 degrees for 8 to 10 minutes. Cool on wire racks. Makes 3 dozen.

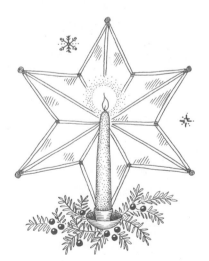

Gifts that feel like a winter wonderland…after filling gift boxes, wrap each in blue paper and then cut out white snowflakes and glue on. Top the package off with a big white bow!

Gingerbread Cookies in a Jar

Karen Cassell
Shalimar, FL

Everyone loves gingerbread...you can't go wrong
with this gift from your kitchen!

3-1/2 c. all-purpose flour,
   divided
1 t. baking soda
1 t. baking powder
1 c. brown sugar, packed

2 t. ground ginger
1 t. ground cloves
1 t. cinnamon
1 t. allspice

Mix 2 cups flour with baking soda and baking powder; place in a one-quart, wide-mouth jar. Add brown sugar to jar, packing down tightly. Mix remaining flour with ginger, cloves, cinnamon and allspice; add to jar and secure lid. Attach a gift tag with baking instructions.

Instructions:

Empty jar contents into a large mixing bowl; mix well. Add 1/2 cup softened butter, 3/4 cup molasses and one slightly beaten egg; mix until completely combined. Cover and refrigerate for one hour. Roll dough to 1/4-inch thickness on a lightly floured surface. Cut into shapes with cookie cutters. Place cookies on a lightly greased baking sheet; bake at 350 degrees for 10 to 12 minutes. Makes 1-1/2 dozen.

An easy way to add ingredients to jar mixes is to use a tart or jar mix tamper. As each layer of ingredients is added, use the tamper to pack them in tightly...ideal!

Ooey-Gooey Homemade Caramels

Denise Actis
Spring Valley, IL

Wrapped in wax paper, these are an old-fashioned favorite.

14-oz. can sweetened condensed milk	3 c. brown sugar, packed
	2 c. corn syrup
1 c. margarine	1/4 t. vanilla extract

Combine first four ingredients in a heavy saucepan; bring to a boil over medium heat until mixture reaches the soft-ball stage, or 234 to 243 degrees on a candy thermometer. Stir in vanilla and heat for 2 to 3 additional minutes. Pour mixture into a buttered jelly-roll pan and let set. Cut into one-inch squares; wrap each in wax paper. Makes 4 to 5 dozen.

Give homemade goodies in a cheery peppermint striped pail...it's easy! Just add wide red and white stripes of acrylic paint to a clean, dry pail. Let dry, then coat with a protective sealer.

Chocolate Cake Mix in a Jar

Heather Gunsch
Billings, MT

*Give with a container of frosting and some colorful sprinkles
for a gift that's sure to make any busy mom happy!*

3 c. all-purpose flour
2 c. sugar
2 t. baking soda

3 T. baking cocoa
2 t. salt

Sift together all ingredients and pour into a one-quart, wide-mouth jar. Secure lid and attach baking instructions with a gift tag.

Instructions:

Pour jar contents into a large bowl; make 3 holes in mixture. Pour one teaspoon vanilla extract in one hole, 3/4 cup vegetable oil in another hole and 2 tablespoons white vinegar in the last hole. Pour 2 cups cold water over the entire mixture and mix well. Pour batter into an ungreased 13"x9" baking pan; bake at 350 degrees for 30 to 40 minutes or until center tests done. Serves 10 to 12.

Turn silver-plated spoons into sweet jar mix name tags. Wash, dry and spray the bowl of each spoon with metal primer. Use acrylic paint to add names and holiday designs; let dry. Attach to jars with decorative ribbon.

A Holly Jolly Christmas

Million-Dollar Pound Cake in a Jar

Patsy Sye
Statesboro, GA

*These make great teacher gifts...or make a batch and put them in a
pretty decorated basket to give to drop-in guests.*

2 c. butter, softened
3 c. sugar
6 eggs
4 c. all-purpose flour
3/4 c. milk

1 t. vanilla extract
1 t. almond extract
10 1-pint canning jars and lids,
    sterilized

Cream butter until smooth. Gradually add sugar; beat until light and
fluffy. Add eggs, one at a time, beating after each addition. Add flour
alternately with milk, beginning and ending with flour. Stir in vanilla
and almond extracts. Spray jars with non-stick vegetable spray with
flour; pour batter into jars, filling each halfway. Wipe rims clean and
place jars on a heavy baking sheet. Bake at 325 degrees for 40 to
45 minutes. Remove any excess cake over jar rims; immediately place
sterilized lids on top and secure. Place jars on a wire rack to cool;
check lids for seal. Makes 10 jars.

*Jar mixes are sure to be a welcome teacher gift and will
get an A+ with a clever blackboard label. Cut a square
of heavy black paper and add the teacher's name using
a fine-point white marker. Secure to the front of the jar
with spray adhesive...ready in minutes!*

Overnight Coffee Cake in a Jar

Denise Shaw
Drexel Hill, PA

An ideal gift for a holiday hostess…she'll love to make it Christmas morning.

1/2 c. sugar
1 c. brown sugar, packed
   and divided
4 T. buttermilk powder
2 c. all-purpose flour
1/2 t. baking soda

1/2 t. salt
1 t. baking powder
1 t. cinnamon, divided
1/2 t. nutmeg
Optional: chopped nuts

In a one-quart, wide-mouth jar, layer sugar, 1/2 cup brown sugar, buttermilk powder, flour, baking soda, salt, baking powder and 1/2 teaspoon cinnamon, packing down tightly after each addition. Combine remaining brown sugar, remaining cinnamon, nutmeg and chopped nuts in a small plastic zipping bag; label as "topping." Place bag on top of ingredients in jar. Secure lid and attach baking instructions.

Instructions:

Remove topping mix from jar; set aside. Empty jar ingredients into a large mixing bowl; blend with a whisk. Add 2 eggs, 2/3 cup melted butter and one cup water; blend with an electric mixer for 3 minutes. Pour batter into a 13"x9" baking pan coated with non-stick vegetable spray; cover and refrigerate 8 to 12 hours. Uncover and sprinkle topping mix evenly over batter. Bake at 350 degrees for 30 to 35 minutes. Serves 8 to 10.

A shimmering welcome…set tea lights inside frosted juice glasses. So pretty along a walkway or on porch steps.

Christmas Morning Cappuccino Mix
Jennifer Clingan
Dayton, OH

Slip a jar into a stocking for an early morning treat.

2/3 c. instant coffee granules
1 c. powdered sugar
1 c. powdered non-dairy
    creamer
1 c. chocolate drink mix

1/2 c. sugar
3/4 t. cinnamon
3/8 t. nutmeg
2 12-oz. jars and lids

Blend coffee granules until fine; place in a large bowl and add remaining ingredients. Stir until well mixed. Divide mixture between the 2 jars; secure lids and attach instructions. Makes 2 jars.

Instructions:

Mix 3 tablespoons cappuccino mix with 3/4 cup hot water or milk. Makes one serving.

Spoon Christmas Morning Cappuccino Mix into plastic zipping bags and tuck inside mugs with holiday designs. Keep several in a basket by the door…so handy for drop-in guests.

Peanut Cookie Brittle

Sandy Bernards
Valencia, CA

Candy or cookie? It's the best of both!

1 c. sugar
1 c. butter, softened
1/2 t. salt
1 t. vanilla extract

2 c. all-purpose flour
1 c. salted peanuts
1 c. semi-sweet chocolate chips

Combine sugar, butter, salt and vanilla in a large mixing bowl; beat with an electric mixer for 2 to 3 minutes on medium speed. Reduce speed to low and add flour; beat until well mixed. Stir in peanuts and chocolate chips. Press mixture into a lightly greased jelly-roll pan. Bake at 375 degrees for 15 to 25 minutes or until edges are golden; cool completely. Drizzle glaze over top. Cut into bars or break into irregular pieces. Makes 4 dozen.

Glaze:

1 c. powdered sugar
2 T. creamy peanut butter

3 T. hot water

Stir together sugar and peanut butter; gradually stir in water to desired glazing consistency.

Give a vintage-style lunchbox filled with homemade cookies…the lunchbox makes a great gift long after the cookies are gone!

⭐ A Holly Jolly Christmas

White Chocolate Chip Jar Cookies

Sharon Pruess
South Ogden, UT

Macadamia nuts make these cookies an extra-special holiday treat.

1/2 c. sugar
1/2 c. chopped macadamia nuts
1 c. white chocolate chips
1 c. brown sugar, packed

2-1/2 c. all-purpose flour
1 t. baking soda
1/4 t. salt

Layer sugar, nuts, white chocolate chips and brown sugar in a one-quart, wide-mouth jar, packing down tightly after each addition. Combine flour, baking soda and salt in a small bowl; add to jar. Secure lid and attach a gift tag with baking instructions.

Instructions:

Empty cookie mix into a large bowl; stir to combine. Add 3/4 cup softened butter, one slightly beaten egg and one teaspoon vanilla extract. Mix until completely blended. Shape dough into one-inch balls and place on a non-stick baking sheet. Bake at 350 degrees for 10 minutes. Makes 2-1/2 dozen.

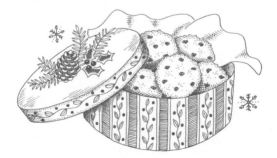

A plate of cookies makes a yummy gift, and here's an easy way to make them extra-special. After placing the cookies on a plate, just drizzle melted chocolate over both them and the plate...so pretty!

Orange-Pumpkin Loaf

Brad Daugherty
Gooseberry Patch

My family gives this often as holiday and housewarming gifts.
Try substituting dates for the raisins for a whole new taste.

1 orange
1/3 c. butter, softened
1-1/3 c. sugar
2 eggs
1 c. canned pumpkin
1/3 c. water
2 c. all-purpose flour

1 t. baking soda
1/2 t. baking powder
3/4 t. salt
3/4 t. cinnamon
1/2 t. ground cloves
1/2 c. chopped walnuts
1/2 c. raisins, chopped

Leaving peel on, cut orange into wedges; remove seeds. Place orange with peel in a food processor; pulse until finely chopped. Set aside. Cream butter and sugar in a large bowl until smooth; beat in eggs, one at a time. Stir in pumpkin, water and processed orange. In a separate bowl, sift together flour, baking soda, baking powder, salt, cinnamon and cloves; stir into batter until just moistened. Fold in walnuts and raisins. Spoon batter into a well-greased 9"x5" loaf pan. Bake at 350 degrees for one hour or until a toothpick inserted near the center comes out clean. Let stand 10 minutes, then remove to a wire rack to cool completely. Wrap in plastic wrap when completely cooled. Makes one loaf.

Make giftwrap fun...tuck loaves of sweet bread inside
big, over-size Christmas stockings!

Holiday Stollen

Caroline McGaha
Knoxville, TN

Shortly after Thanksgiving my family gets ready to make Holiday Stollen. This started with my great-grandmother and has continued for 5 generations. Everyone takes turns stirring the dough in a very large tub, and after about 15 cups of flour Grandpa and Dad come in to help! Be sure to get out the biggest bowls you've got!

8 c. plus 4 T. sugar, divided
4 T. shortening
3 T. salt
4 c. hot water
8 pkgs. active dry yeast
3 c. warm water
9 lbs. all-purpose flour, divided
4 c. butter, melted
1 qt. milk
12-oz. can evaporated milk
1 c. cold water

4 lbs. raisins
1 lb. currants
2 lbs. mixed candied fruit
1/2 lb. green candied cherries, halved
1/2 lb. red candied cherries, halved
1 T. cinnamon
3 T. lemon extract

Combine 4 tablespoons sugar, shortening, salt and hot water in a large bowl. Dissolve yeast in warm water; add to mixture. Stir in 8 cups flour. Cover bowl and let stand for 5 to 6 hours. Blend in butter, milk, evaporated milk and cold water. Stir in raisins, currants, mixed fruit, cherries, cinnamon, remaining sugar, lemon extract and remaining flour. Cover dough with a towel and let sit overnight. Divide dough in half and let rise until double in bulk. Knead dough and divide into 30 loaves; place into lightly greased 9"x5" loaf pans. Cover pans and let dough rise. Bake at 350 degrees for 40 to 50 minutes or until centers test done. Cool on wire racks. Wrap each loaf in aluminum foil. Makes 30 loaves.

Double Chocolate Surprise Cookies

Karla Ihrke
Owatonna, MN

You'll find a yummy chocolate drop hidden in each cookie!

12-oz. pkg. chocolate chips
1/4 c. butter
14-oz. can sweetened
   condensed milk
1 t. vanilla extract

2 c. all-purpose flour
60 milk chocolate drops,
   unwrapped
1/2 c. white chocolate chips,
   melted

Combine chocolate chips and butter in a saucepan; melt over low heat until smooth. In a mixing bowl, stir together milk and vanilla; add chocolate mixture. Stir in flour to form a dough. Wrap a tablespoon of dough around each chocolate drop. Arrange cookies on ungreased baking sheets; bake at 350 degrees for 6 to 8 minutes. Allow to cool. Drizzle melted white chocolate chips over each cookie. Makes 5 dozen.

Add a whimsical touch to a Christmas tree or stack of gifts. Use fabric paint to write the words of a favorite Christmas carol on a long length of wide ribbon. Wrap the ribbon around gifts or use as garland for the tree...fun!

✪ A Holly Jolly Christmas

Tuxedo Brownies in a Jar

Lisa Tatun
Shelton, CT

Tie black & white sheer ribbon around the jar for a first-class gift...great for co-workers.

1/2 c. walnuts
1/2 c. white chocolate chips
1/2 c. chocolate chips
2/3 c. brown sugar, packed

1 c. plus 2 T. all-purpose flour
1/3 c. baking cocoa
2/3 c. sugar
1/4 t. salt

Layer all ingredients in a one-quart, wide-mouth jar, being sure to pack down after each addition. Secure lid and attach baking instructions and a gift tag.

Instructions:

Empty brownie mix into a large bowl. Add 3 eggs, 2/3 cup oil and one teaspoon vanilla extract. Pour into a greased 9"x9" baking pan. Bake at 350 degrees for 25 to 30 minutes. Cut into squares. Serves 6 to 8.

Arrange white buttons in the shape of a snowflake on top of a wrapped gift, and then glue in place...a clever package topper in minutes!

Christmas Biscotti Mix

Ellie Brandel
Clackamas, OR

I like to give this mix with a baking sheet and holiday pot holders.

3/4 c. dried cranberries or
   cherries
3/4 c. shelled green pistachios
2 c. all-purpose flour

1/2 t. cardamom
2 t. baking powder
2/3 c. vanilla sugar

Layer all ingredients in a one-quart, wide-mouth canning jar, packing down tightly after each addition. Secure lid and attach a gift tag with baking instructions.

Instructions:

Beat 1/3 cup butter in a large mixing bowl on medium speed for 30 seconds. Add 2 eggs and beat on medium until well combined. Stir in jar mix until blended. Form dough into two, 9"x2" loaves on a lightly greased baking sheet. Bake at 375 degrees for 25 to 30 minutes; cool on sheet for one hour. Cut each loaf into slices 1/2-inch thick. Arrange slices on baking sheets and bake at 325 degrees for 8 minutes; turn each over and bake 8 to 10 additional minutes or until dry and crisp. Cool on a wire rack. Makes 2 to 3 dozen.

Homemade vanilla sugar couldn't be easier! Just pour 4 cups sugar into a one-quart jar. Slice one vanilla bean in half lengthwise and add both halves to the sugar. Secure jar lid and allow to sit for 2 to 3 weeks. Makes 4 cups.

A Holly Jolly Christmas

Cookie Dough Truffles

*Kathy Price
Quincy, MI*

Drizzle with melted raspberry chips for a delicious finishing touch.

1/2 c. butter, softened
1/2 c. brown sugar, packed
1/4 c. sugar
1/4 c. refrigerated egg substitute
1 t. vanilla extract
1-1/4 c. all-purpose flour

1 c. mini semi-sweet chocolate
   chips
3/4 c. chopped walnuts
12-oz. pkg. semi-sweet
   chocolate chips
1-1/2 T. shortening

Beat butter with an electric mixer on medium speed until creamy; gradually add sugars, beating well. Blend in egg substitute and vanilla. Gradually add flour, beating well. Stir in mini chocolate chips and walnuts. Cover dough and chill for 30 minutes. Shape mixture into one-inch balls; cover and freeze until firm. Place chocolate chips and shortening in a one-quart glass bowl; melt in the microwave in 20-second intervals until smooth. Using 2 forks, quickly dip frozen truffles into melted chocolate, coating completely; place on wax paper to harden. Keep refrigerated up to 3 days. Makes 4-1/2 dozen.

Instead of giving sweets in a candy dish, layer colorful candies in a tall glass vase. Simply cover the top with clear cellophane, tie with bright curling ribbons and add a gift tag.

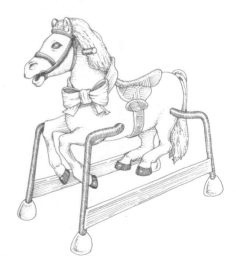

4-Berry Spread

Jana Tate
San Antonio, TX

Pair this with a warm loaf of bread for a gift that's sure to get raves.

1 c. blackberries
1 c. blueberries
1-1/2 c. strawberries, hulled
1-1/2 c. raspberries
1-3/4 oz. box powdered fruit
   pectin

7 c. sugar
7 1/2-pint canning jars and
   lids, sterilized

Crush berries in a heavy stockpot; stir in pectin. Bring mixture to a rolling boil over high heat, stirring constantly. Stir in sugar; return to a full rolling boil. Boil for one minute, stirring constantly. Remove from heat; skim off any foam. Pour mixture into hot jars, leaving a 1/4-inch space at the top; secure lids. Process jars in a boiling water bath for 10 minutes. Makes 7 jars.

Jars of jams and jellies look sweet with Christmas bulb gift tags. Use a paint pen to write names on colorful plump Christmas light bulbs and secure around jar neck with a pipe cleaner.

Holiday Cranberry Jam

Donna Reid
Payson, AZ

After the jars are cool, I place a piece of Christmas fabric over the lid of each jar to add a festive touch.

2 c. cranberries
1 orange, peeled and divided
    into sections
16-oz. pkg. frozen strawberries,
    thawed

3 c. sugar
3 oz. liquid fruit pectin
5 1/2-pint canning jars and
    lids, sterilized

Coarsely grind cranberries and orange sections in a food processor; spoon into a heavy stockpot. Add strawberries and sugar. Bring mixture to a full rolling boil over high heat, stirring constantly for one minute. Remove from heat and stir in pectin. Skim off any foam and immediately pour into hot jars; secure lids. Process jars in a boiling water bath for 10 minutes. Makes 5 jars.

If someone's celebrating a birthday during the holidays, tuck several jars of homemade jam in a tin picnic basket that's been lined with colorful vintage fabric. A gift that's sure to be remembered!

Lotsa Pepper Jelly

Teresa Hill
Lima, NY

Attach a festive card to each jar with serving suggestions such as:
Spoon Lotsa Pepper Jelly over cream cheese-topped crackers;
use as a glaze on roast turkey or ham or mix a few tablespoons
with sour cream for a tangy vegetable dip.

2 green peppers	6 oz. liquid pectin
1/2 c. chile peppers	7 1/2-pint canning jars and
1-1/2 c. cider vinegar	lids, sterilized
6 c. sugar	

Remove stems and seeds from peppers; discard. Grind green peppers in a food processor until liquefied. Measure 3/4 cup processed peppers into a heavy saucepan. Grind chiles until liquid and add to pan; stir in vinegar and sugar. Bring mixture to a full rolling boil, stirring constantly. Add pectin and stir until well blended. Bring back to a full rolling boil and boil for one minute. Remove from heat and skim foam. Spoon into hot jars and seal. Process in a boiling water bath for 5 minutes. Makes 7 jars.

Fill a rustic basket with jars of Lotsa Pepper Jelly, crackers, cream cheese and bandanna napkins for a one-of-a-kind gift. Create labels and jar toppers using colorful beads and fabrics tied on with jute to add a southwestern feel!

A Holly Jolly Christmas

Zesty Steak Sauce

Wendy English
Jacksonville, FL

I have been making this for Christmas gifts for years. By May and June, I usually have people asking for more!

12-oz. bottle chutney
2 14-oz. bottles catsup
10-oz. bottle steak sauce
5-oz. bottle Worcestershire
     sauce

hot pepper sauce to taste
4 1-pint jars and lids

Place chutney in a blender or food processor and process until chopped but not smooth; mix with remaining ingredients. Pour mixture into jars and seal; store in refrigerator. Makes 4 jars.

Sweet & Tangy Mustard

Hope Davenport
Portland, TX

Give a bag of pretzels with this tasty dip.

14-oz. can sweetened
     condensed milk
8-oz. jar mustard

2 T. prepared horseradish
2 T. Worcestershire sauce

Stir all ingredients together; spoon into an airtight container. Refrigerate up to 3 months. Makes 3 cups.

Parmesan-Garlic Popcorn Spice

Bonnie Weber
West Palm Beach, FL

Everyone in my office seems to be snacking on popcorn every afternoon. I gave this spice to them last year and they loved it!

1/2 c. grated Parmesan cheese   1 t. garlic powder
2 t. salt   1 t. dried parsley
1 t. dried tarragon

Combine all ingredients in a small bowl; stir until well blended. Store in an airtight container. Give with instructions for serving. Makes 1/2 cup mix.

Instructions:

To serve, melt 1/4 cup butter in a small saucepan over low heat. Stir in one tablespoon popcorn spice. Pour over 3 cups popped popcorn; stir well.

Pop up a fun family gift! Fill a big enamelware bowl with bags of popcorn, salt, recipes for snackable popcorn treats, a classic Christmas video and a jar of Parmesan-Garlic Popcorn Spice.

⭐ A Holly Jolly Christmas

Tex-Mex Spice Mix

*Michael Davenport
Portland, TX*

With so many uses, this will be a hit with everyone on your list!

3 T. chili powder   1 T. salt
2 T. cumin   1 T. garlic powder
1 T. pepper   1-1/2 t. red pepper

Mix all ingredients together and store in an airtight container. Attach a gift card with instructions. Makes 1/2 cup mix.

Instructions:

Sprinkle to taste on chicken, beef, potatoes, corn and popcorn.

Seasoning Salt

*LaVerne Fang
Joliet, IL*

Shake on garlic bread, salads, subs, pasta, chicken or hamburgers...wherever you'd like a little extra flavor.

1 c. salt   1 t. onion powder
1 t. dried thyme   1 t. curry powder
1 t. dried oregano   2 t. dry mustard
1 t. garlic powder   2 t. paprika

Blend together all ingredients. Store in an airtight container. Makes 1-1/4 cups mix.

Harvest Bean Soup Mix

Elizabeth Talmage
San Clemente, CA

The beans look really pretty layered in an old-fashioned glass jar.

1/4 c. dried lentils
1/4 c. pearled barley
1/4 c. dried green split peas
1/4 c. dried black-eyed peas
1/4 c. dried lima beans
1/4 c. dried baby lima beans

1/4 c. dried red beans
1/4 c. dried pinto beans
1/4 c. dried white beans
1/4 c. dried Great Northern
   beans

Combine all ingredients in an airtight container. Attach a gift tag with cooking instructions.

Instructions:

Wash beans in a bowl of cold water, removing any that float to the top. Cover with fresh water and soak overnight. Drain, rinse and place in a large stockpot with 2 quarts water; add chopped ham if desired. Bring mixture to a boil; lower heat and simmer 4 hours, stirring frequently. Add a red pepper pod, 2-pound can of tomatoes, a chopped onion, juice of one lemon, one teaspoon chili powder, salt and pepper to taste. Simmer 20 additional minutes. Serves 12.

Mixes don't always have to be given in jars...spoon them into a retro-style canister, soup tureen or red speckled stockpot!

A Holly Jolly Christmas

Spicy Pickle Slices

Christine Watt
Kempton, PA

Set a jar inside a napkin-lined basket and then tie a pickle fork to the basket handle.

2 32-oz. jars dill pickle slices,
  drained
4 c. sugar
1 T. hot pepper sauce

1/2 t. red pepper flakes
3 cloves garlic, peeled
3 1-pint jars and lids

Combine pickles, sugar, pepper sauce and red pepper in a large bowl; mix well. Cover and let stand at room temperature for 2 hours, stirring occasionally. Spoon mixture into jars. Add a garlic clove to each. Secure lids and refrigerate one week before giving. Makes 3 jars.

It's Christmas in the mansion,
Yule-log fires and silken frocks;
It's Christmas in the cottage,
Mother's filling little socks;
It's Christmas on the highway;
in the thronging, busy mart.
But the dearest, truest Christmas,
is the Christmas in the heart.
-Unknown

Cinnamon-Applesauce Ornaments

Heather Muckley
Berlin, NJ

Decorate ornaments with ribbon, bows, buttons and paint.
I've made these sweet shapes into pins too...just glue on
a pin back once the ornaments have dried.

1/3 c. cinnamon
1 t. ground cloves
1 t. nutmeg

1/4 c. applesauce
2 t. craft glue

Combine spices in a small bowl; add applesauce and glue. Knead mixture until a smooth dough forms. Roll dough to 1/4-inch thickness between 2 sheets of plastic wrap. Remove top wrap and cut dough with cookie cutters. Use a straw to cut a hole in the top of each ornament, if desired. Place shapes on a wire rack to dry. Dry for 3 to 4 days, turning each day. Makes 12 to 15.

A quick holiday kitchen decoration...tuck cinnamon ornaments along with fresh greens into a big antique apothecary jar. Add some fabric ticking-striped candy canes for a vintage look.

A Holly Jolly Christmas

Apple-Spice Simmering Potpourri

Gwen Stutler
Emporia, KS

Fresh apples and oranges make this simmering potpourri smell heavenly!

1 apple
1 orange
4 cinnamon sticks

4 bay leaves
8 whole cloves

Wrap each ingredient in plastic wrap or tulle. Place all ingredients in a gift box lined with tissue paper, or tuck inside a fabric bag with a holiday print. Tie on a gift tag with instructions.

Instructions:

Cut orange and apple into 1/4-inch slices. Add half of all ingredients to 2 to 3 cups water in a saucepan; bring to a boil. Reduce heat and simmer. Refresh aroma by adding water and remaining ingredients as needed.

All the goodies that make up this simmering potpourri could be tucked inside a watering can (for a friend who loves gardening) or a holiday cookie jar (for a baker)...they'll love it!

Holiday Placemats

Patti Greger
Lititz, PA

Every year my kids recycle the pictures from the Christmas cards we receive. They put them in a big plastic bag and put them away with the Christmas decorations. When we get decorations out the following year, the kids find their bags, a 14"x11" piece of construction paper and glue sticks. Each of them make a holiday collage with their Christmas card cut-outs. We then cover each side with clear contact paper, trim the edges with pinking shears and they have their own special placemats for December!

Goodie Bag

Michelle Stanton
Little Rock, AR

For a quick & easy goodie bag, cut colorful construction paper the same width as a plastic zipping bag, making the length 3 inches. Fold construction paper in half, lengthwise, so it is now the width of the bag and 1-1/2 inches long. Stamp a holiday design on one side. Fill the bag with homemade cookies or candies, jelly beans or mints. Seal the bag and place the paper over the seal, so that it is folded over the bag. Staple closed and add "To" and "From" on the back!

⭐ A Holly Jolly Christmas

Christmas Mailbox

Teree Lay
Sonora, CA

As a fun holiday surprise for my grandchildren, I decided to spruce up a mailbox using holiday stencils, fabric, greenery and bows; then I filled it with fun little trinkets collected throughout the year. Whenever my grandchildren stop at Grammee's during Christmas, the first thing they do is check to see if they have mail...of course, they always do!

Santa Gift Bag

Susan Winstead
Chicago, IL

Cut a piece of white paper in a square that just fits into a clear plastic zipping bag. Before fitting the paper into the bag, add 2 round stickers to make eyes on the square and one sticker to make a nose. Use a red crayon to draw on a mouth and rosy cheeks and a black crayon to make a few long wavy lines to form a beard. Slip the Santa inside the bag and fill the bag with candies. To finish the gift bag, cut a piece of red paper in a triangle to make Santa's hat. The bottom of the triangle should be wide enough to just cover the top of the plastic bag. Glue a white cotton ball to the point of the triangle, seal the bag and tape the hat to the top.

Give handmade Christmas stockings extra charm...use a vintage tea towel for the stocking cuff!

Snowball Candle

Lynne Gasior
Struthers, OH

In Ohio, we usually have snow for Christmas, but to guarantee a white Christmas, I make snowball candles. Just buy a bag of wax beads, a candle boiling bag and a round candle. You can find all these at craft stores. Pour about 1/4 of the beads in the boiling bag, make sure there isn't any water inside the bag, and tie the bag closed with a twist tie. Fill a stockpot 3/4 full of water; add the bag of wax beads and heat it over medium-low heat until the wax is melted. Open the bag carefully and pour the wax into a heat-proof bowl. As it cools, it will begin to form a film on top. When the wax is still liquid, but the film is starting to form, whip the wax with a fork or whisk until it becomes fluffy. Begin to spoon the warm wax onto the round candle, pressing the wax on but leaving it rough looking. Using a fork to press it on helps give it a rough texture. While the wax is still warm, sprinkle snowball candle with glitter. After the wax hardens, shake off any excess glitter and you will have a sparkling snowball!

Pile lots of Snowball Candles in a tin pail and set by the door. As guests leave, they can take their pick from the bucket of snowballs!

⭐ A Holly Jolly Christmas

Frosty Ice Candle

Paula Zsiray
Logan, UT

My mother and I made these beautiful candles and their soft glow was the only light my family would have Christmas Eve.

To make one, wash and dry a cardboard one-pint milk carton; use a utility knife to cut away the top of the carton. Place a taper in the center of the carton, trimming the bottom of the candle, if necessary, so it's just below the top of the carton. Use sticky wax squares (available at craft stores) to secure the taper in the bottom of the carton; set aside. Heat one inch of water in the bottom of a double boiler. Remember that wax is flammable, so continue to add water to the double boiler as needed...don't melt wax in a pan placed directly on a burner. Place an empty coffee can in the water; reduce heat to simmer. Add a 9-ounce package of wax beads to the coffee can. Use a craft stick to stir wax as it melts.

Crush ice into small pieces and arrange around the taper in carton. Before ice melts, carefully pour the melted wax into the carton; do not cover wick. Set aside until all the wax has hardened and then invert it over a sink to drain the water. When the candle has cooled, peel away the milk carton and place the candle in a pie pan to catch any drips when the candle is lit. You can easily make larger candles using a 1/2 gallon cardboard milk carton.

For lots of sparkle, set a plump candle in a clear dish and surround it with rock candy!

Primitive Christmas Pictures

Traci Ippolito
Industry, PA

Here's my way of creating primitive-style Christmas pictures while preserving my children's artwork. I used my 3-year-old's first drawing of a snowman (3 circles and some squiggly arms) because it had the perfect primitive look. To create this, you will need a child's drawing, muslin, a picture frame, embroidery floss and transfer paper. Cut muslin about one inch larger than the frame. If you'd like, soak muslin in strong tea for a really aged look. Use transfer paper to transfer the drawing onto muslin, and then use embroidery floss to chain stich the picture and place it in the frame. Don't forget to write the child's name and age somewhere on the frame for a sweet, heartfelt keepsake.

Festive Paper Cones

Sharon Clement
Winslow, ME

Lay a paper plate on a flat brown paper bag; trace around the plate to form a circle. Cut out the circle, using decorative-edged scissors if you'd like, then cut from one edge of the circle to the center. Twist the paper into a cone and glue the edges. Fill the cone with tissue paper to just below the upper edge, and glue ribbon ends to the inside edge of the cone (at opposite sides) creating a loop for hanging. Glue holly berries to the tissue paper, mounding them over the top of the cone or fill the cone with fresh greenery or homemade candy. Hang on neighbors' doors for a delightful holiday surprise.

✦ A Holly Jolly Christmas

Bella Basket

Katie Spangler
Jasper, GA

One of my favorite gifts to give a busy hostess or friend during the holiday season is a "Bella Basket." It's a quick gift that provides a fast, delicious meal for a family on the go. Just fill a basket with a loaf of Italian bread, a jar of pasta sauce, a box of pasta and a jar of Parmesan cheese. You can even leave out the bread and put in a gift certificate to the local bakery for a fresh-baked loaf. Be sure to tuck in a CD of holiday music and a bottle of sparkling cider before wrapping it all up in a red checkered tablecloth…a gift sure to be remembered!

Recipe Magnets

Maile Helekahi
Honolulu, HI

Last Christmas I made recipe magnets for my friends & family. I chose my favorite homestyle recipes, typed them on the computer and printed them out on decorative paper. I then decoupaged the recipe to a square tile, took them to a well-ventilated area and sprayed each tile with a coat of clear sealer. Once the sealer was dry, I hot glued a heavy-duty magnet to the back of each tile . Everyone was so happy to get these as gifts because I usually make these tried & true recipes for them once a year…now they can make them whenever they want!

Fill a child-size purse with fun…candy necklaces,
lipsticks, watches and chocolate coins.
Any little girl will love it!

Hearthside Pine Cone Baskets

Jenn Vallimont
Kersey, PA

Arrange pine cones in a pretty basket using hot glue. Begin by placing large pine cones in the bottom to fill it up quickly. Once you've reached the top, use smaller, more unique pine cones. Try to arrange the pine cones so it looks like they've fallen; some upside-down and on their sides. It's nice to have one or 2 "spilling" over the edge. Once they're all arranged, just tie a holiday bow on the handle. These are beautiful sitting beside the fireplace or as centerpieces, and they are always welcome gifts!

Sentimental Tree Skirts

Robin Lutz
Cranberry Township, PA

Use old quilts and blankets from your children's nursery as tree skirts. Just wrap around the bottom of the tree and you'll have a nostalgic, country touch in no time.

Transform an ordinary terra-cotta pot saucer into a terrific gift in minutes. Simply hot glue peppermint candies around the rim and when dry, set a votive in the center surrounded with more candies.

☆ A Holly Jolly Christmas

Sugar Plum Pillowcases

Penny Sherman
Cumming, GA

It's so quick & easy to dress up plain pillowcases, that when family & friends are coming for a Christmas visit, I always make several for the guest room. Begin by washing and ironing each pillowcase. Then, using a sponge brush, add an even coat of permanent fabric paint to a rubber stamp. Firmly press the rubber stamp onto the pillowcase; let dry. Set the design by tumbling pillowcases in a warm dryer for 20 minutes. To add variety, I like to use lots of rubber stamp designs...snowmen, candy canes, stars and Christmas trees are a few of my favorites and they can be easily cleaned using window cleaner and water.

Pinwheel Wreath Ornament

Sharon Diehl
Emmaus, PA

Make the prettiest wreaths in just minutes! Buy bags of round peppermint candies in both green & white and red & white. Unwrap the candies and place them in tart pans in a circle around the edge. Place pans in a 350-degree oven for 2 to 3 minutes or until the candy melts together forming wreaths; remove promptly. As soon as they are completely cooled, pop them out of the pans onto sheets of newspaper or parchment paper. Attach a green or red ribbon and hang for beautiful tree ornaments, window decorations or package tie-on's.

For a whimsical glow, nestle a dripless taper inside a canning jar that's filled halfway with colorful hard candies or buttons.

Country Candles

Cyndy Rogers
Upton, MA

Clean a one-pint canning jar and let dry. Fill the jar 1/3 of the way with dried green split peas. Fill the next 1/3 with yellow corn kernels, and then insert a beeswax taper into the center. Fill around the taper to the top with dried red lentils and tie a plaid ribbon around the jar. They make such pretty centerpieces and hostess gifts. I've made several over the seasons and always receive compliments on such an easy but attractive country Christmas decoration!

Stocking Twist

Lisa Ragland
Gooseberry Patch

When I was younger, instead of hanging up stockings, my family hung children's footed pajamas by the fireplace. The covered feet kept the gifts inside, and it always added a sweet look to the room!

Family photos make terrific gift tags. Just copy, cut out and tie on. And there's no need to write "To" on each tag…everyone can open the packages with their picture!

Cinnamon Bunch Ornament

Michelle Campen
Peoria, IL

Glue 8 to 10 cinnamon sticks together and tie a festive red ribbon around the middle. Embellish the ribbon with a sprig of greenery and berries and attach a green or red cord around the ribbon for hanging on a tree…looks really cute tied on a package too!

Jar of Thank-You's

Michelle Kirk
Hampton, VA

A couple years ago, I gave my mom a "jar of thank-you's." I decorated a glass canning jar with stickers and ribbons and then filled it with about 100 strips of paper on which I had thanked my mom for all the little things she did to make my life so wonderful. I included things like "Making orange juice popsicles for me and my friends," "Letting me have slumber parties," "Making snickerdoodles," "Encouraging me when I was away at college," and "Adjusting my veil on my wedding day." Christmas morning, she read a few aloud and was so moved that she saved the rest to read on her own. She told me later that day that it was the best gift I had ever given her.

For the prettiest party gifts, tie sheer ribbon bows through the hanger on glittery blown glass ornaments and then place one at each table setting.

Snowman Kit

Aryn Lentz
Camp Hill, PA

When first moving into our neighborhood, my family wanted to give presents to all the kids, so we got creative! Because we live in a snowy area, we made snowman kits. We painted wooden dowels orange for the carrot noses, painted bottle lids black for the coal eyes and buttons and cut fabric into long strips for scarfs. We tucked everything into decorated cardboard tube containers and personalized each with the child's name. On the bottom we wrote "Happy Holidays" and signed our names. That winter it was such fun for my kids to see the familiar snowmen all around the neighborhood.

Holiday Surprise Boxes

Amanda Dixon
Gooseberry Patch

For a fun-filled surprise, wrap a small gift inside a gift box. Then wrap the box in another box, and keep going until you have several wrapped boxes within wrapped boxes! It's really fun to watch the "grand opening." Of course, you'll want the final gift to be extra special!

For a reminder that Santa's on his way, wire a length of sleigh bells to a fresh greenery wreath...a jolly jingle every time the door opens!

Remember *When?*

Valerie Orleans
Anaheim Hills, CA

One of my favorite memories involves creating a holiday treat with my then 4-year-old daughter, Raisa. Despite my challenges with crafts, I decided that my daughter and I should attempt to create a gingerbread house. Knowing my creative limitations, I opted for a "pre-fab" kit...the kind where the gingerbread pieces are already baked and cut.

So on a crisp December morning, Raisa and I began to assemble our gingerbread house. First we got 2 sides up...so far so good. I proceeded to "glue" wall 3 when wall 2 began to slump. We straightened it and proceeded to wall 4. Once the final wall was up, the others began to tilt. This went on for some time before we finally got all 4 sides to stand...then there was the roof. A few attempts and the entire house collapsed. At one point, in complete and total frustration, I looked at my daughter and asked, "How about gingerbread ruins? Anyone can have a gingerbread house, you'll have something different!" She wasn't buying it.

After several more attempts, we managed to get the house (which looked more like a shanty) to stand. My daughter then began to decorate with pounds of gumdrops, peppermints, licorice sticks, wafers and candies. By the time we finished, it looked like a joke...frosting everywhere, candies scattered and the house looked like it would collapse if you stared at it too long.

I was about ready to toss the whole mess out when my daughter whispered, "Isn't it the prettiest house you've ever seen? And we made it!" Nobody would ever suggest that our gingerbread house would win any blue ribbons, but to my daughter it was a glorious achievement. And what she taught me that year was that it was the effort and time we spent together that was important...not whether or not the gumdrops were lined up in a perfect row.

Remember When?

Sarah Fore
Springfield, IL

Every Christmas Eve when I was growing up, my dad, mom, sister and I drove into town to my grandparents' house where we were joined by my aunt, uncle and cousins. We had such fun eating, chatting and, of course, opening presents. One particular year, when my sister and I were young, it was quite foggy outside during our drive back home out in the country. My dad saw the red light on the top of the TV tower near our house. He woke my sister and me up (we always fell asleep on the way home!) and told us that if we looked out the window, we could see Rudolph! We looked and there it was...a bright red light in the midst of all the fog. We knew it was Rudolph's nose and we were so excited! What joy in being a child during Christmas. I'll always remember this special, fun memory.

Delinda Blakney
Canton, GA

A very treasured tradition at our home is the Blessing Basket. Our special basket sits in our family room. Throughout the year when we have been blessed, we write the blessing on a slip of paper and drop it into the basket. Sometime between Christmas and New Year's Eve we have a meaningful family night and enjoy a special meal or activity which we end with the readings from our Blessing Basket. It is a wonderful way to remain focused on the goodness of life and keeps us "counting our blessings" all year long.

Jane Anderson
Dowagiac, MI

My special memory occurred some years ago, but I remember it well. My family had recently moved into a large Victorian home, and my husband and I, along with our 3 sons, had gone to the local tree farm looking for a large tree to place in the tower of one of our parlors. The owner showed us 2 perfect blue spruces. We picked our favorite and the kids danced around while we cut down the tree. The great outdoors can be deceiving as far as size, but we managed to get it into the owner's truck and up to our station wagon. Since it was too heavy to lift off the ground, we rolled it from the truck bed on top of the car and tied it down.

Once we were home, we realized we couldn't get it in the house by ourselves. We called some neighbors over, and after needing to run out for a large stand, we finally got the tree up! The branches swept the sides and ceiling of the 9-foot wide tower and it looked wonderful. I felt like a child myself and so grateful for the help of our friends. My husband Andy, however, had placed himself behind the tree to help steady it up and he was stuck! As the others held the tree in place to keep it from tipping, Andy crawled under the branches.

We had pizza and cocoa and became very excited to trim the tree. It took hours putting all our ornaments on the tree, and Andy and I reminisced about where and when we got the decorations. We were lucky that an old wooden 10-foot ladder was left with the house because it came in handy for trimming the upper areas. Andy even had to use a yard stick to place some ornaments on the top branches. The tree was the crown that completed the picture of the first Christmas in our old home and I'll never forget that experience.

Remember When?

Dawn Harvey
Island, KY

My mother has always taught me that family is the best source of joy if you allow it to be. When she was a little girl, the family always cut down their Christmas tree right from the woods and brought it to the house to decorate. My grandmother had told my uncles, who were teenagers at the time, not to cut down a tree that was too tall so it would look nice in their living room. Mom says that they brought home a tree that was so tall it bent over at the ceiling and came back down the tree halfway to the ground. The sweet part is that they left it that way, decorated it, and created a wonderful holiday memory that my mother has passed on to me. What a wonderful gift to have a Christmas laugh in memory of my uncles and their tree.

Caroline Booth
Salt Lake City, UT

Last Christmas, my mother-in-law told all of her children and their spouses that she and my father-in-law did not want any of us to buy them gifts for Christmas in the coming years. Instead, she wants us to do a good deed for someone in need during the holidays. We'll write it down on a piece of paper, put it in an envelope and place it on the tree. On Christmas morning, they will open all the envelopes and read aloud the good deeds that were done in the spirit of Christmas. What a wonderful tradition!

Barbara Beahan
Coral Springs, FL

Each fall, I send an invitation to 7 close friends for our annual Christmas Cookie Exchange. We have been sharing holiday treats for many years and it is an occasion that is eagerly anticipated each year. Since there are 8 of us, each person brings 8 individually wrapped cookies or candies; 7 are swapped with others and one is enjoyed that evening. In addition, each person brings a Christmas ornament or decoration for a grab bag. We've found that everyone has such fun and searches year 'round for something special to bring! I always prepare a favorite punch along with flavored coffee to enjoy as we sample the treats, and then we play a game to distribute the ornaments and decorations. What a treat to enjoy this special evening shared with treasured friends.

Nancy Hauer
Rifle, CO

Throughout the Christmas season I sing Christmas carols to my children as I tuck them in bed or rock them to sleep at night. There's never been a more beautiful lullaby than *Silent Night* sung softly in the darkness. This tradition takes me back to the time when my wonderful parents sang with our family. Although my parents are gone now, I feel them with me as I sing these special songs to their grandchildren and I hope that one day my children will enjoy this same feeling of closeness with their own children.

Remember When?

Dorothy Boyson
Austin, TX

During one of our annual Christmas Eve celebrations, my son-in-law seated each family member in front of the large, decorated Christmas tree and interviewed them with his video camera. He asked them to tell their name, age, how they fit into the family and what they remembered of Christmases from their early childhood years. The participants ranged in age from 4 to 90 years and the stories that were told brought laughter and tears.

Ninety-year-old Aunt Kitty told of her visits with grandparents and enjoying tea parties with small porcelain dishes. My mother remembered her early years in Texas with no money for buying a tree or wrapping paper...she picked a pretty holly tree with red berries, added pieces of cotton for trim and drew pictures on brown bags to make wrapping paper. My brothers remembered our early years and the gifts found (and secretly used) before Christmas, and then acting so surprised when they found them under the tree Christmas morning. My nephew told of singing carols in Aunt Dot's kitchen with Uncle Wilbur. It was a wonderful evening with family gathered for eating, exchanging gifts, singing and reminiscing.

Kelly Gardner
Grafton, VA

My mother and I have held a Christmas-in-July party for the past 6 to 7 years. It started out just the 2 of us, wrapping some early purchases and listening to holiday music. Now it has expanded over the years to quite a celebration! We invite our family & friends sometime around July 25th for an all-day party. We fill the room with Christmas decorations, play Christmas movies and music and even turn up the air-conditioning to get that "cool" holiday feeling. Everyone comes dressed in holiday attire, and they bring crafts to work on for the season. If they need some inspiration, I set up craft stations around the room where they can go and try something new. Everyone also brings a new holiday dish they want to try out so we can test new recipes, get wrapping done and start on all those crafts that are waiting to be completed. It's tons of fun!

Kristine Smith
Hampton, NJ

Each Christmas Eve when my daughter was young and I knew she was fast asleep, I carefully painted footprints across the kitchen floor leading to where she had left a plate of cookies for Santa and carrots for the reindeer. Each Christmas morning she was amazed at how those "elf" footprints were always there!

Remember When?

Amy Arnsperger
Salisbury, MO

My favorite memory of Christmas has to do with family silliness and sacrifice. I grew up in a small town in northwestern Missouri. My mother's family was from St. Louis. Every holiday season, we would make the trip to see them before Christmas, but always made sure we would be back at our house Christmas morning. One year, when I was about 8 years old, it began to snow on the morning of Christmas Eve. It snowed steadily all day, making it seem impossible for us to head home. My dad, however, insisted that we get on the road…so through a blinding snowstorm we struggled. The trip took us 2 hours longer than usual, but it was worth it. My little brother, who was 3 years old at the time, stayed up almost the whole way home watching for Santa and his reindeer. About a mile from our house, he finally caved in to his exhaustion, just as a herd of deer ran across the road in front of us! The rest of us laughed as we were pulling in the driveway and headed off to bed. The next morning we awoke to a tree full of presents and an exhausted set of parents. Not only did they drive home in the bad weather, they also stayed up the rest of the night putting together all the gifts!

Thanks for the snack!
Love,
Santa

Nicolena Hensler-Gordon
Oconomowoc, WI

My favorite Christmas memory takes me back to the year my "baby brother" was 3 years old. I was the oldest of the 4 children in my family and my brother the youngest. It was with great certainty that year, at age 7, that I was sure there was no Santa Claus. Christmas morning, my brother woke us all up so excited that he had just seen Santa downstairs by the tree! I knew that it had to be my uncle who was coming over later that day to play Santa. My parents, however, were still in bed and no one had been up to let my uncle inside. We found a little piece of fuzzy red felt snagged on the tree, and we all decided then and there that Santa was real. To this day, even though my brother is no longer a baby but a college student, we can all say, "I believe in Santa," because we really do.

Gail Shackelford
Martinsburg, WV

Every year since my son was a toddler, I have helped him choose several toys he no longer plays with to leave by the front door for Santa to take to children who might not have as fortunate a Christmas holiday. His dad or I then take the toys to our local charity organization. He's 8 years old now, and this really encourages him to shift his focus away from the "give me, give me" aspect that Christmas sometimes takes on for small children. Instead, he's thinking of others whose Christmas might not be as bright as his. It's terrific to see him thinking how Christmas is a time for giving to others.

Remember When?

Rita Pilis
Franklin, MA

This is not a single memory, but a recurring memory from my childhood, especially dear to me now that both my parents are gone. Each year, as we enter the month of December, I remember that sweet day that I would come home from school to find my father in the living room, painstakingly assembling our artificial Christmas tree, with all the color-coded branches strewn around the room!

All the rest of our Christmas decorations were up, having been done by my mother while I was at school...our stockings were hung by the fireplace, the little white table-top tree with the white angel lights was set up in the family room and our beautiful manger was sitting atop the television. I would always run to my room, hoping I'd find my big Santa pillow, which only appeared for the holiday season, upon my bed. I was never disappointed!

Helping my dad assemble the tree, with Christmas music playing in the background, and the smell of Mom's bread baking in the kitchen was heaven on Earth. The reward was when the evening came, and we turned off all the lights and illuminated the Christmas tree. I would sit under that tree for hours, with the warmest feeling of love and happiness.

I have tried to recreate that feeling for my children with our own special traditions and decorations, plus a few precious decorations I have from my parents. Savor the season, but most of all, savor your family and every day together, for this is the greatest gift of all!

Michelle Black
Greeley, CO

All my life, I've dreamed of a white Christmas, but living in Southern California really lowered my chances. So, in 1992, when I had a chance to move, I picked Colorado, knowing that I would have that white Christmas. As the first Christmas approached, I was disappointed to learn that we would not be getting any new snow and I would have to make do with what we already had. During the next 7 years, I never gave up hoping it would snow on Christmas Day. I always imagined waking up Christmas morning to find a winter wonderland.

During Christmas 2000, my husband and I were celebrating our second Christmas together in our brand new home and my whole family came to spend the night. Christmas Eve was full of magic as we each took turns adding little gifts to stockings, wrapping last-minute presents and ending the evening sitting by the Christmas tree listening to Mom read the Christmas story from the Bible. When I went to bed, I looked outside but saw no sign of snow.

I slept fitfully that night, but my excitement woke me up about 6:30 in the morning. My husband got out of bed first and went to the window to check on our dog. He calmly told me to come look outside…I thought I was dreaming because it was snowing. A white Christmas at last! I raced across the hall into the guest room where my mom was still in bed, and I pulled up the blinds. Soon my husband, mom, brothers and their girlfriends were all piled on the bed staring out the window. We were all silent as we watched the snow fall to the ground. I had never seen a more beautiful morning in all my life. It was a winter wonderland!

Remember When?

Krista Pikitus
Girardville, PA

I come from a very small, close-knit family so I have many fond memories from childhood. One of my favorite memories was passing the presents on Christmas Eve. Every Christmas Eve after mass, my parents, grandparents, my sister and I would line up along the staircase and pass the Christmas gifts down one by one. It was always fun waiting to hear what my father thought was contained in the boxes...he had an idea about every one! My sister always had the job of stacking the presents under the tree. The last 2 presents passed were the gifts that my sister and I were able to open that night, which were always our Christmas pajamas. We then hung our stockings and we all sat down to watch a Christmas movie together. The only presents yet to arrive were the ones from Santa Claus! This tradition continued even after we both were married. We all still gather at my parents' house on Christmas Eve to pass the presents. My sister and I both have children now and we are looking forward to continuing this tradition with our daughters. Hopefully, it will become one of their most cherished memories as well!

Marsha Dixon
Bella Vista, AR

My greatest memory of Christmas was when I was growing up in Clinton, Iowa. Every Christmas Eve, we would drive around looking at Christmas decorations on the houses. Every time we would all get in the car, my dad would have to go in the house to find the car keys. We would then drive around and look at the lights, and when we got home Santa had already been to our house. We would have our gifts on Christmas Eve and were able to play with them. Then, on Christmas morning, my mom and dad were able to sleep in! I always wondered what took Dad so long to get his car keys.

MariDee Wittl
Woodbury, MN

My mom would take my brother and me to mass on Christmas Eve. My dad would stay at home to "take a nap." When we would return from church, we would find reindeer tracks in the snow and a trail of candy and small gifts to the Christmas tree, so we knew Santa had arrived. Every year, my dad would claim that Santa was as quiet as a mouse because he didn't awaken from his nap!

Remember When?

Mindy Gehring
Bedford, TX

Being far away from home during the Christmas season, our family doesn't have the privilege of having family gatherings during the holidays. So we came up with the idea a few years ago to gather with other neighborhood families in the same situation. We hop into our van, drive through neighborhoods decked out with lights and sing all the old traditional Christmas songs that we sang as kids. Some of us sing off key, some of us forget the words, but it just adds to the fun. We always finish the evening by reading *'Twas the Night Before Christmas*. So even though we are all apart from our families at Christmas, we are together in spirit and in heart!

Wanda Scott Wilson
Hamilton, GA

When I decided to use a bare-branched sweet gum tree, covered in "snow," instead of a Christmas tree, I tried for weeks to remember how my talented mother, who passed away many years ago, made snow out of common household ingredients. No one in our family could remember either! The day before friends were coming to lunch, I sat down, slightly panicked, to eat my breakfast toast and picked up a cookbook that happened to be lying on the kitchen table; it was a book I never used and had placed in a stack to donate to a charity. The book fell open to the very page that told how to mix 2 cups Ivory Snow with 1/2 cup water to make "snow." "Thank you Mama," I said, "That was close!"

Elisabeth Lutz
Budd Lake, NJ

When our sons were still at home, we would choose a "Christmas Elf." On November 30th, we would each draw the name of the person for whom we would be an elf; this was kept a secret until Christmas day. Then every day until the 25th, we would do something nice for the person…throw their dirty clothes in the hamper, leave a piece of candy for them or secretly do a chore for them. On the 25th, we would reveal ourselves to them with a note and a small but meaningful gift.

Jennifer DeGraw
Redmond, OR

My family has created a very special tradition that we share at Christmas time. My husband and I take our son to the humane society on the the 23rd of December with a box of dog treats and a can of cat treats. He gives each dog and cat a treat and leaves the extras to be passed out later. This allows us to share some of our love with animals who don't have anyone to love them.

Remember When?

Cathy Howell
Farmington, IL

One of my favorite Christmas memories was when I was about 6 years old. Dad was a city policeman and Mom stayed at home to care for their 5 children. I can remember the last few days before Christmas and Mom's old blue and white speckled turkey roaster filled with cut-out sugar cookies. Money was tight back in the 1950's and sweet decorated cookies were a once-a-year treat. I remember the cut-out bells, trees and stars all decorated in blue, green and yellow frosting with little red and silver candy decorations and colorful sprinkles. I remember Mom saving her aluminum pie tins all year for this occasion to put cookies in and give to friends & family who stopped by. Even people she didn't know very well always got a gift of cookies and a smile. To this day, I think of those Christmas cookies every time I smell sugar cookies baking or see an old blue turkey roaster.

Barbara Smith
Sikeston, MO

For 13 years now, my family has made an advent cookie tree to prepare for the celebration of the birth of Jesus. On Thanksgiving weekend, we prepare our cookie dough and bake our favorites…bar cookies seem to hold up best in flavor and freshness. The times I spend in the kitchen with my husband and daughter are priceless. Everyone is involved! We package the cookies in plastic zipping bags and hang them on a flat, green wooden tree. As we take off each night's cookie dessert, we replace it with a cross-stitch ornament that I made for our tree. This is the highlight of our season. I can't imagine celebrating without our cookie tree!

Maria McGovern
Stratford, NJ

When my husband Paul and I were first married, we had little money (as most couples do when they first start out) and we were saving for a house. What we did have were 14 nieces and nephews to buy Christmas gifts for. What we decided to do was have a sleepover at our home! The children would all come have pizza for dinner and then we would make Christmas ornaments or hand-made presents for their parents. Incidentally, the sleepover was a gift to the moms and dads too. You see, our brothers and sisters used this night to "Santa" shop while we had all the children! We would have a great time singing Christmas carols and watching our favorite Christmas programs like "Scrooge" and "How the Grinch Stole Christmas." That was 10 years ago and most of the children are out of school, but they still come over to our house just to be with each other during the holiday season.

Lynn Ferguson
Lockport, NY

To kick off the holiday season, my daughter, husband and I spend Thanksgiving evening watching a classic Christmas movie and stringing popcorn and cranberries for our tree. The secret to making it last is to use stale popcorn that has been popped 3 to 5 days before and left out. We also use fishing line and a large darning needle and make lots and lots of strands for a glorious country Christmas tree!

Remember When?

Alexis Mauriello
Richardson, TX

When I was a child, living in the northeast, Christmas was usually snow-covered and beautiful. One Christmas, when I was 8 years old, my grandmother came to visit a little earlier than expected due to the weather prediction. She arrived a day or so earlier and was planning to stay through the New Year's celebration. My fondest memory is of my grandmother, an Italian immigrant who could not read or write and who spoke in broken English, cooking and baking up a storm in our kitchen with my mother. On Christmas Eve, in the evening, some carolers braved the snowstorm and were singing at our front door. My grandmother welcomed them inside to warm up for a few minutes and have some hot chocolate. About 2 hours later, after they had eaten cookies, candies, homemade pizza, espresso coffee and hot chocolate, they went happily on their way. The image of that Christmas Eve returns to me every Christmas and always brings a smile to my face.

Stacey Weichert
Waseca, MN

One of my fondest memories is of lying beneath Grandma and Grandpa's shiny aluminum Christmas tree and watching the reflection of the rotating electric light wheel on the beautiful glass ornaments.

Pat Ghann-Akers
Bayfield, CO

One of our most memorable Christmas celebrations was when our family spent a week on a snow-covered mountain in California. We had the opportunity to make cookies and candies, take sleigh rides, go to church on Christmas Eve and sing carols with the locals. We even cut down our own tree! Luckily, the cabin we rented had an A-frame ceiling or else we would've never gotten it inside! The only store-bought decorations on the tree were the lights. All other ornaments were handmade by the adults and children. We had colored paper chains, clay handprints, pine cones from outside and of course, strings of popcorn and cranberries.

I think this Christmas stands out in our children's memories as one of the best, even though we did not buy lots of gifts for one another. Being together in such a beautiful place was the best gift we could have received.

Remember When?

Christa Kerr
DuBois, PA

Every December, beginning soon after Thanksgiving, Santa would "fly by" our house to see if my brother, sisters and I were being good. We always knew he had come to check our behavior because we heard his sleigh bells ring as he flew past the window. As we grew older we realized that Santa always came to check on us when Dad went out to do barn chores or fix the fire. Even though they no longer live on the farm, Dad kept the sleigh bells and repeated this ritual for his grandchildren, except with a twist. The house they live in now is a long ranch-style home with a full-length attic, perfect for Santa to stomp on the roof and "Ho, Ho, Ho" to the delight of every grandchild. At least once each Christmas, my daughters still recall the "paw prints" on the roof. I hope in a few years Dad can carry on the tradition with his great-grandchildren.

Tammy Young
St. Peters, MO

Every year during the last few days before Christmas, we make a new "Memory List." The list has questions that stay the same, but with 4 children, our answers differ each year. Some examples of questions are: favorite food, favorite song, best friend, teacher and what you want to be when you grow up. We also add a new question every year. As we write our new list, we review the old year's answers. We laugh and laugh and it's a highlight of mine that I wait for each year.

Jennifer Smith
Manchester, CT

My grandmother has a journal that she has had for as long as I can remember. Every year at Christmas this journal is brought out and set next to her chair in the living room. This journal contains memories from Christmases in our family for the past 20 years. Each year, we take turns reading through the pages, each of us remembering something different as we look through.

After looking the book over, we each try to write a little something about this year's happenings so that we can reflect on them again in the coming years. This year, I get to write about my first baby's first Christmas. And someday I know that she will be able to look back and read exactly how I was feeling that day. I think that's pretty special.

Sylvia Weiser
Myrtle Creek, OR

It was Christmas, 1969 and my husband had been stationed in Vietnam since February. He was not due to come home until the following February. He had written home and said not to send any goodie packages until after the holidays, as he was due to go to Australia for his R & R. My 3 boys, ages 9, 4 and 17 months, and I were feeling rather blue, but were doing the best we could. Then on December 22nd (my husband's birthday) I received a call from him saying he would be home just as soon as he could catch a cab from the airport! His R & R had been cancelled and he received orders to go home instead! It was a big surprise and made for a very special Christmas.

'Tis the Season

...e Ball

Cheri Emery
Quincy, IL

...ahead snack is great when unexpected guests drop by.
Keep one in the refrigerator...just in case.

2 8-oz. pkgs. cream cheese, softened	1 T. Worcestershire sauce
8-oz. pkg. shredded sharp Cheddar cheese	1/2 t. salt
	1/4 t. celery salt
	1 c. chopped pecans

Blend together all ingredients except pecans. Cover and chill 3 hours, then shape into a ball. Roll in pecans. Keep refrigerated until serving. Serve with assorted crackers. Makes 8 to 10 servings.

Christmas Punch

Kathy Unruh
Fresno, CA

Colorful and oh-so delicious.

2 qts. cranberry juice	2 qts. ginger ale
juice of 4 lemons	Garnish: orange slices and
1 qt. orange juice	maraschino cherries
1/2 c. sugar	

Mix together first 4 ingredients in a large bowl; pour into a punch bowl over ice. Add ginger ale. Garnish with orange slices and cherries. Makes about 6 quarts.

Tasty tip...make an ice ring of fruit juice to keep punch from becoming diluted!

'Tis the Season

Cranberry Cocktail Meatballs

Dawn Hankwitz
West Allis, WI

Not only delicious, they're easy to make too...another
good reason to try them!

2 lbs. ground beef
3 eggs
1-1/2 oz. pkg. onion soup mix
1 c. bread crumbs
1-1/2 c. chili sauce

1-1/2 c. water
2 c. sauerkraut
2 c. cranberry sauce
1 c. brown sugar, packed

Mix together ground beef, eggs, soup mix and bread crumbs. Form mixture into one-inch balls; arrange in an ungreased shallow baking pan. Bake at 350 degrees for 20 to 30 minutes or until cooked through; drain well. Combine remaining ingredients in a mixing bowl; pour over meatballs and continue to cook at 350 degrees for 1-1/2 hours. Makes 5 dozen.

It's easy to add a warm glow to any holiday
get-together with lots of twinkling lights and candles!

Deviled Egg Delights

Elizabeth VanEtten
Warwick, NY

For a holiday touch, slice a green olive with pimento
and place on each egg.

12 eggs, hard-boiled and peeled
2 T. onion, chopped
1 t. horseradish sauce
1 t. mustard
3 T. mayonnaise

2 T. sweet pickle relish
1/8 t. salt
1/8 t. pepper
1/8 t. sugar
Garnish: paprika

Cut each egg in half and place the yolks in a mixing bowl. Add remaining ingredients to egg yolks; beat with an electric mixer until thoroughly combined. Fill egg whites with yolk mixture. Sprinkle tops with paprika. Makes 2 dozen.

Instant Christmas cheer in any room...just fill a
red enamelware pan with a forest of
bottle-brush trees.

'Tis the Season

Hot Reuben Dip

Karrie Middaugh
Salt Lake City, UT

All the flavor of a delicious sandwich in a tasty dip!

14-oz. can sauerkraut, rinsed
 and drained
1-1/2 c. shredded Cheddar
 cheese

1-1/2 c. shredded Swiss cheese
1 c. corned beef, chopped
1 c. mayonnaise

Pat sauerkraut with paper towels to absorb extra moisture. Combine all ingredients in a large mixing bowl. Spread in an ungreased 1-1/2 quart casserole dish. Bake at 350 degrees for 25 minutes or until hot and bubbly. Serve with sliced rye or baguette bread. Serves 15 to 20.

Fondue pots do double-duty for more than just fondue. They're ideal for keeping dips or meatballs warm.

White Pizza Dip

Lisa Ashton
Aston, PA

This one's always a hit!

1-1/2 oz. pkg. herb with garlic
   soup mix
8-oz. container sour cream
8-oz. container ricotta cheese

1 c. shredded mozzarella cheese
1/4 c. chopped pepperoni
1-lb. loaf Italian bread, cubed

Combine all ingredients, except bread, in an ungreased 1-1/2 quart casserole dish. Bake at 350 degrees for 30 minutes. Serve with bread cubes. Serves 10 to 12.

3-Cheese Italian Dip

Jenny Henry
Inwood, WV

Add pepperoni, sausage, onion or peppers for variety.

8-oz. pkg. cream cheese,
   softened
1 t. Italian seasoning

1 c. shredded mozzarella cheese
3/4 c. grated Parmesan cheese
8-oz. jar pizza sauce

Mix together cream cheese and Italian seasoning; spread in the bottom of an ungreased 8"x8" baking pan. Combine cheeses in a small bowl; sprinkle half the mixture over cream cheese. Spread pizza sauce over cheese; top with remaining cheese mixture. Bake at 350 degrees for 15 to 18 minutes or until bubbly. Serve with toasted bread, crackers or vegetables. Serves 10 to 12.

Keep buffet table decorations easy...small pastry tins can double as candle holders for glitter-dusted votives.

'Tis the Season

Sausage Bites

Judy Cheatham
Brentwood, TN

Fill a basket with these tempting appetizers to share with co-workers...you're sure to take home an empty basket!

1 lb. ground sausage, browned
2-2/3 c. all-purpose flour
2 T. sugar
1 t. baking powder
1/2 t. baking soda
1/2 t. salt

1 T. active dry yeast
1/4 c. warm water
1 c. buttermilk
1/2 c. oil
1/4 c. butter, melted

Set sausage aside to cool. Combine flour, sugar, baking powder, baking soda and salt in a mixing bowl; set aside. In a separate bowl, dissolve yeast in warm water; mix with buttermilk and oil. Add yeast mixture to dry ingredients. Stir in sausage. Cover and chill for one hour. Roll dough out on a floured surface; cut with a biscuit cutter and arrange on a baking sheet coated with non-stick vegetable spray. Bake at 425 degrees for 10 to 15 minutes. Brush tops with melted butter. Makes 12 servings.

Use copies of vintage wrapping paper, gift tags, stickers and stamps to make one-of-a-kind party invitations.

Bacon-Wrapped Jalapeños

Vickie

Use banana peppers instead for a yummy mild version.

20 jalapeño peppers
8-oz. pkg. cream cheese

20 bacon strips, halved
crosswise

Cut peppers in half lengthwise; remove stem and all seeds. Stuff each half with 2 teaspoons cream cheese. Wrap a bacon strip around each pepper and secure with a toothpick. Arrange peppers on a broiler rack coated with non-stick vegetable spray. Bake at 350 degrees for 20 to 25 minutes or until bacon is crisp. Remove toothpicks and serve warm. Makes 40.

Mexicalli Dip

Judy Garcia
Las Vegas, NV

A recipe first shared with me over 15 years ago by a co-worker;
I find people are still surprised to learn what the ingredients are!

2 T. butter
2 eggs
2 16-oz. cans chili with beans
15-1/2 oz. can hominy, drained

16-oz. pkg. Mexican-style
pasteurized process cheese
spread, cubed

Heat butter in a skillet; add eggs and scramble. Stir in chili and hominy; simmer for 20 minutes. Gradually add cheese, stirring until melted. Serve with tortilla or corn chips. Serves 10 to 12.

Quick as a wink...just toss a colorful quilt on the buffet table for a terrific tablecloth!

'Tis the Season

Festive Holiday Spread

Bea Hegarty
Gilbert, AZ

Arrange crackers around this tasty spread and watch it disappear!

8-oz. pkg. cream cheese,
   softened
4-oz. can chopped black olives
4-1/2 oz. can chopped green
   chiles

1 bunch green onions, chopped
16-oz. container sour cream
1 tomato, chopped

Blend together cream cheese, olives, chiles and onions. Place spread on a serving platter and form into a candy cane shape. Cover with plastic wrap and chill; remove 15 minutes before serving. Spread sour cream over spread. Sprinkle tomatoes over sour cream to form stripes. Serve with assorted crackers. Makes 10 to 12 servings.

Create a sugarplum swag using beads, balls, baubles and bows in beautiful vintage colors. The pinks, greens, purples and blues are so pretty on a greenery garland!

Cheesy Artichoke Dip

Lisa Mayfield
Branchburg, NJ

*Serve this straight from the oven so the cheese is warm
and melted when guests dig in.*

2 15-oz. cans artichoke hearts
1 c. mayonnaise
1 c. Parmesan cheese
2 t. garlic powder

8-oz. pkg. shredded mozzarella
  cheese
Garnish: paprika

Drain artichoke hearts and squeeze between paper towels to remove excess moisture. Chop artichokes and blend with remaining ingredients. Spread mixture in a greased 9" round baking pan. Bake at 350 degrees for 25 minutes. Sprinkle paprika over top. Serve with crackers or tortilla chips. Makes 10 to 12 servings.

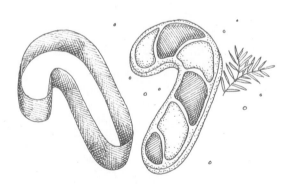

Just for fun, use cookie cutters to spell out holiday
greetings on a cupboard shelf or mantel. It's easy to
keep them in place with poster tape.

Pimento-Broccoli Dip

Mary Ann Nemecek
Springfield, IL

Vegetables and crackers taste great with this dip too.

10-oz. pkg. frozen chopped
   broccoli, thawed
1 c. sour cream
1 c. mayonnaise
2 T. chopped green onions
2 T. fresh parsley, chopped

2-oz. jar diced pimentos,
   drained
1/2 t. dill weed
1/4 t. salt
1/8 t. garlic powder
1-lb. loaf French bread

Use paper towels to squeeze out excess moisture from broccoli. Finely chop broccoli and set aside. In a small bowl, combine sour cream and mayonnaise; stir in broccoli and remaining ingredients, except bread. Cover and chill for 2 hours. Slice off top crust from French bread; hollow out the inside and cut removed bread into cubes. Place bread cubes on an ungreased baking sheet; bake at 350 degrees for 8 to 10 minutes. Spoon dip into hollowed-out loaf. Serve with toasted bread cubes. Serves 10 to 12.

Clever party favors! Remove the caps from clear glass ornaments, then write holiday greetings on pieces of paper no wider than the ornament. Roll up each greeting, slip inside the ornament and replace the cap. Remember to keep the paper small so it can unroll easily after it's tucked inside the ornament.

Blue-Ribbon Chicken Fingers

Jackie Balla
Walbridge, OH

*A prize-winning appetizer when dipped in ranch dressing,
honey mustard or hot barbecue sauce.*

6 boneless, skinless chicken
   breasts
1 c. milk
2 T. vinegar
1 egg, beaten
1 t. garlic powder

1 c. all-purpose flour
1 c. seasoned bread crumbs
1 t. salt
1 t. baking powder
oil for deep frying

Cut chicken into 1/2-inch strips; place them in a large plastic zipping
bag. Combine milk and vinegar together in a small bowl; add egg and
garlic powder. Pour milk mixture over chicken in bag; seal and
refrigerate 4 to 6 hours. In a separate plastic zipping bag, combine
remaining ingredients. Drain chicken, discarding milk mixture. Place
chicken in flour mixture; seal bag and shake to coat. Heat oil in an
electric skillet to 375 degrees. Fry coated chicken strips on each side
for 4 to 5 minutes or until golden. Place on paper towel to drain.
Serves 6 to 8.

For Christmas trees
that twinkle, hang lots
of sparkly chandelier
prisms from
the branches.

'Tis the Season

Christmas Eve Tidbits

Karen Hoag
Jackson, NE

A couple hours before Christmas Eve dinner, my family sets out a table full of snacks and treats...we call it "tidbit time."

1/2 c. butter, melted	1 t. salt
3 eggs	1 t. baking powder
1 c. milk	16-oz. pkg. shredded Pepper
1 c. all-purpose flour	Jack cheese

Pour melted butter into a 13"x9" baking pan, tilting to coat the bottom. Use an electric mixer to combine eggs, milk, flour, salt and baking powder. Stir in cheese. Pour batter into buttered pan; bake at 350 degrees for 20 to 25 minutes or until golden. Cut into small squares. Makes about 4 dozen.

Placecards in a snap! Tape a placecard to the wire loop at the top of a tree ornament, and then lay at each place setting. Guests can take the ornament home as a reminder of all the fun they had.

Loaded Baked Potato Skins

Gloria Kaufmann
Orrville, OH

No one can resist biting into these...they're wonderful!

4 potatoes, baked
3 T. oil
2 T. grated Parmesan cheese
1/4 t. salt
1/4 t. garlic powder
1/4 t. paprika
1/8 t. pepper

8 slices bacon, crisply cooked
   and crumbled
1-1/2 c. shredded Cheddar
   cheese
1/2 c. sour cream
4 green onions, chopped

Cut potatoes in half lengthwise; scoop out centers, leaving 1/4 inch around the edges. Reserve centers for another recipe. Place potato skins on a greased baking sheet skin-side up. Combine oil, Parmesan cheese, salt, garlic powder, paprika and pepper; brush over skins. Bake at 475 degrees for 7 minutes. Turn skins over, brush with oil mixture and bake an additional 7 minutes. Sprinkle bacon and cheese inside skins; bake 2 more minutes or until cheese is melted. Top each with cream cheese and onions. Makes 8.

Country candles that are so easy to make! Fill the bottom of a canning jar with holly or boxwood, place a handful of fresh cranberries on top and add water to just below the jar rim. Top it off with a floating candle...beautiful!

'Tis the Season

Sausage-Stuffed Mushrooms
Jo Ann

If you like a little more kick, try using hot sausage...just as delicious!

1 lb. mushrooms
1/2 lb. ground sausage
1/4 c. onion, chopped
1/3 c. catsup

2 T. bread crumbs
1 t. dried parsley
1/2 t. dried basil

Remove stems from mushrooms; finely chop enough stems to measure 1/2 cup. Crumble and cook sausage in a large skillet. Stir in mushroom stems and onion; cook until sausage is browned, stirring frequently. Drain mixture and place in a mixing bowl; stir in catsup, bread crumbs, parsley and basil. Fill each mushroom cap with mixture. Arrange mushrooms on an ungreased baking sheet; bake at 375 degrees for 12 to 15 minutes. Makes 2 to 3 dozen.

A wreath of holiday cookie cutters makes a sweet welcome! Arrange cutters on a flat surface, secure them with paper clips or fine-gauge silver wire and top with a big bow.

Savory Cheesecake

Marilyn Rogers
Port Townsend, WA

*Take a new spin on cheesecake with this appetizer version.
To serve, cut in thin wedges and spread on crackers
or toasted French bread.*

2 T. butter, melted
6-oz. pkg. cheese crackers,
    crushed and divided
1/2 c. stuffed green olives,
    chopped
1/2 c. celery, chopped
1 onion, chopped
2 T. lemon juice

1 t. salt
1 t. Worcestershire sauce
1/4 t. paprika
1/8 t. hot pepper sauce
2 c. sour cream
Garnish: pimento strips and
    olives, sliced

Brush the bottom and sides of a springform pan with melted butter.
Cover the bottom of the pan with half the crushed crackers. In a
separate bowl, mix together olives, celery, onion, lemon juice, salt,
Worcestershire sauce, paprika, hot pepper sauce and sour cream.
Spread mixture over cracker crust; sprinkle remaining crushed crackers
over top. Cover pan and refrigerate 24 hours. Garnish top with
pimento and olives. Serves 8 to 10.

*Use rubber stamps to add a jolly design to solid-color
giftwrap. What a simple way to make any gift
more special!*

'Tis the Season

Santa's 5-Layer Dip

Jackie Goodnight
Elizabethtown, NC

A ho-ho-holiday hit!

8-oz. pkg. cream cheese
1 onion, chopped
2 T. olive oil
16-oz. can refried beans
4-1/2 oz. can chopped green
   chiles

8-oz. jar taco sauce
8-oz. pkg. shredded Mexican
   cheese blend

Spread cream cheese in the bottom of an ungreased 13"x9" baking pan; set aside. Sauté onion in olive oil in a skillet until tender; stir in refried beans. Spread bean mixture over cream cheese. Layer green chiles and taco sauce over bean mixture; sprinkle cheese over top. Bake at 325 degrees for 15 to 20 minutes or until cheese is melted. Serve with tortilla chips. Makes 15 to 18 servings.

There are no bells in all the world so sweet
as sleigh bells over snow.
-Elizabeth Coatsworth

Shrimp & Crabmeat Spread

Kathleen Kosinski
West Mifflin, PA

A terrific blend of flavors.

8-oz. pkg. cream cheese,
    softened
1/2 c. mayonnaise-type salad
    dressing
4-1/2 oz. can salad shrimp,
    drained

1/3 c. onion, chopped
1/8 t. garlic salt
6-oz. pkg. crab meat, drained

Combine cream cheese and salad dressing in a serving bowl; mix
until well blended. Stir in remaining ingredients. Cover and chill 2 to
3 hours. Serve with assorted crackers. Makes 2 cups.

For a heartfelt winter warmer, dress up plain hats and
mittens! Cut snowflakes or stars from washable felt,
then attach with embroidery floss using a simple
straight or blanket stitch.

'Tis the Season

Crescent Cheese Rolls

Cathy Jackson
Iona, ID

*These are the best appetizers and they're so quick
to make...and quick to disappear!*

2 8-oz. tubes refrigerated
   crescent rolls
2 4-1/2 oz. cans chopped
   green chiles

12-oz. pkg. shredded Cheddar
   cheese
garlic powder and grated
   Parmesan cheese to taste

Roll out crescent rolls and flatten into 2 rectangles, sealing all
perforations. Spread chiles and cheese over dough. Sprinkle with
garlic powder and Parmesan cheese to taste. Roll up each rectangle,
jelly-roll style, starting at the long ends. Cut both rolls into one-inch
slices; place slices on a lightly greased baking sheet. Bake at
375 degrees for 12 to 15 minutes. Makes 1-1/2 to 2 dozen.

Make the countdown to
Christmas a treat!
Hide trinkets in goodie
bags or hang wrapped
gingerbread men
on an advent
calendar...terrific ways give
the kids something to look
forward to each day.

Mom's Cranberry Tea

Heather Bartlett
APO AE, Germany

Mom kicks off the holiday season with this delicious tea...and it makes the house smell great!

3 cinnamon sticks
30 whole cloves
3-1/2 qts. plus 2 c. water,
   divided
1-lb. can cranberry sauce

2 6-oz. cans frozen orange juice
   concentrate, thawed
1 c. sugar
6 T. lemon juice

Combine cinnamon sticks, cloves and 2 cups water in a small saucepan; bring to a boil and boil for 10 minutes. In a large bowl, combine cranberry sauce, orange juice, sugar and lemon juice; add boiling liquid, straining cinnamon sticks and cloves. Pour mixture and remaining water into a slow cooker and heat on low to keep warm before serving. Makes about 5 quarts.

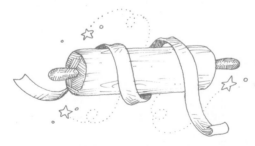

Cranberry Fruit Dip

Tony Horton
Van Buren, AR

This dip looks so pretty on a buffet table.

8-oz. container vanilla yogurt
1/4 t. nutmeg

1/2 c. cranberry-orange relish
1/4 t. ground ginger

Stir together all ingredients until well blended. Cover and chill 2 to 3 hours. Serve with assorted fruits. Makes 6 to 8 servings.

Taffy Apple Dip

Lou Garraway
St. Francisville, LA

Also good with pears and spicy gingersnap cookies.

6 to 8 apples, cored and sliced
pineapple juice
2 8-oz. pkgs. cream cheese,
    softened
1 c. brown sugar, packed

1 T. vanilla extract
12-oz. jar caramel ice cream
    topping
1 c. chopped pecans

Place apple slices in a plastic bag; add enough pineapple juice to coat. Set aside. Mix cream cheese, brown sugar and vanilla with an electric mixer until thoroughly blended; spread into a 9" round pan. Spread caramel topping over top. Sprinkle chopped pecans over caramel. Cover with plastic wrap and refrigerate until serving. Serve with apple slices. Makes 12 to 15 servings.

Don't forget to give windows an extra-special holiday feel. Use red raffia to tie cookie cutters to pine boughs, and then hang over window valances.

Oriental Chicken Wings

Beth Goblirsch
Minneapolis, MN

A constant favorite...on a scale of 1 to 10, these hit the top!

16-oz. bottle soy sauce
1 onion, chopped
1 c. sugar

1 t. ground ginger
5-lb. pkg. frozen chicken wings

Mix together first 4 ingredients in a mixing bowl. Arrange frozen
wings in 2 ungreased 13"x9" baking pans; pour mixture over top.
Bake at 350 degrees for 1-1/2 to 2 hours, turning chicken every
20 minutes. Makes 20 servings.

Pepperoncini-Beef Sandwiches

Carol Hickman
Kingsport, TN

Spread these bite-size sandwiches with creamy horseradish
sauce for even more flavor.

3-lb. beef roast
1-1/2 c. water
16-oz. jar pepperoncini

36 mini croissants
8-oz. pkg. shredded mozzarella
    cheese

Place beef and water in a slow cooker; cook overnight on low heat.
Shred beef and add pepperoncinis with juice; cook on low heat an
additional 4 to 6 hours. When ready to serve, top each croissant with
beef mixture and sprinkle cheese over beef. Makes 3 dozen.

Votive holders sprayed with faux-snow paint set a frosty
scene at any holiday open house.

'Tis the Season

Tangy Buffet Meatballs

Charlotte Smith
Huntingdon, PA

This slow-cooker appetizer makes it ideal for toting to office parties.

2 lbs. ground beef
2 eggs
1/2 t. salt
3/4 c. quick-cooking oats,
    uncooked

1-1/3 c. chili sauce, divided
1/2 c. grape jelly

Combine ground beef, eggs, salt, oats and 1/3 cup chili sauce. Shape mixture into one-inch balls; place in an ungreased shallow baking pan. Bake at 400 degrees for 15 to 17 minutes. Combine grape jelly and remaining chili sauce in a large saucepan; cover and cook over medium heat, stirring occasionally until mixture is well blended. Add meatballs and continue cooking until heated through. Transfer to slow cooker to keep warm while serving. Makes 5 dozen.

Remove the center of cucumber slices with an apple
corer and slide red pepper slices and zucchini
and carrot strips through the holes...a veggie tray
that's anything but boring!

Creamy Parmesan-Chicken Dip

Lisa Willard
Chattanooga, TN

Natural food stores often carry many different flavors of chutney.

8-oz. pkg. cream cheese,
  softened
8-oz. container sour cream
1/2 c. grated Parmesan cheese

12-oz. can cooked chicken
1 to 1-1/2 c. mango chutney
1/2 c. green onions, chopped

Blend together cream cheese, sour cream, Parmesan cheese and chicken in a mixing bowl. Spoon mixture into a 9" round baking pan coated with non-stick vegetable spray. Bake at 350 degrees for 35 minutes or until lightly golden. Remove from oven and allow to sit for 10 minutes. Spread chutney over top and sprinkle with onions. Serve with wheat crackers. Makes 10 to 12 servings.

Stack benches one atop the other for displaying toys, Teddy bears, books and tiny trees that bring back sweet Christmas memories.

'Tis the Season

Golden Sausage-Cheese Balls

Dina Rowan
Eastlake, OH

One taste of these cheesy golden bites and you'll be hooked!

1 lb. ground sausage
1/2 c. water
12-oz. pkg. shredded Cheddar
   cheese

2 c. biscuit baking mix
1 t. baking powder

Combine all ingredients in a mixing bowl; cover and chill overnight.
Roll mixture into walnut-size balls; place on greased baking sheets.
Bake at 350 degrees for 10 to 15 minutes or until golden. Makes
1-1/2 to 2 dozen.

Bread Stick Dippers

Mary Rita Schlagel
Warwick, NY

I like to arrange the bread sticks in a tall glass or vase next to the
dip...easy for guests to grab and dip!

1/2 lb. bacon, crisply cooked
   and crumbled
1 c. sour cream
1 c. mayonnaise

4 to 5 plum tomatoes, diced
   and drained
Garnish: fresh parsley

Mix together bacon, sour cream, mayonnaise and tomatoes in a
serving bowl. Garnish with parsley. Serve with bread sticks. Makes
6 to 8 servings.

Twist a length of garland around napkins for
quick-as-a-wink napkin rings!

Mini Ham Puffs

Mary Dishman
Evansville, IN

These disappear at every party, and they're so easy to make.
To save time, prepare the ham mixture the day before!

2-1/2 oz. pkg. cooked ham,
   chopped
1/2 c. shredded Swiss cheese
1-1/2 t. Dijon mustard
1 egg

1/2 c. chopped onion
pepper to taste
8-oz. tube refrigerated
   crescent rolls

Mix together first 6 ingredients; set aside. Roll out crescent roll dough, sealing all creases and perforations. Use a pizza cutter to slice dough into 24 equal squares. Lightly grease and flour a mini muffin pan; place a square of dough into each muffin cup. Fill each with ham mixture. Bake at 350 degrees for 13 to 15 minutes or until golden. Makes 2 dozen.

Bundle up taper candles with a vintage postcard and then tie them together with ribbon for a gift that's sure to be a hit.

Bacon Roll-Ups

Carolynn Zeitz
Macomb, MI

*My kids really enjoy helping out in the kitchen during the holidays,
and this is one of their favorite recipes.*

10-3/4 oz. can cream of chicken
   soup
1-lb. loaf sliced bread, crusts
   trimmed

1 lb. bacon, halved crosswise

Pour soup in a mixing bowl and stir until creamy. Use a rolling pin to flatten each piece of bread. Brush the soup mixture onto both sides of each bread slice; roll up each slice jelly-roll style. Wrap 2 pieces of bacon around each roll, leaving about one inch between the bacon pieces; cut each roll in half making 2 individual roll-ups. Arrange roll-ups on a broiler pan coated with non-stick vegetable spray. Bake at 400 degrees for 8 to 10 minutes or until bacon is done. Makes 8 to 10 servings.

Make it merry & bright! When decorating with
floating candles, tint the water with
a drop of food coloring.

Janet's Shrimp Ball

Janet Catt
Camano Island, WA

No special occasion or celebration goes by without someone requesting this appetizer.

4-1/2 oz. can salad shrimp, drained
8-oz. pkg. cream cheese, softened
1-1/2 t. minced onion

1 t. seasoned salt flavor enhancer
1/2 t. lemon juice
1 c. chopped pecans

Mix together first 5 ingredients and form a ball. Roll in chopped pecans until covered. Serve with assorted crackers. Serves 10 to 12.

Fabric yo-yos make the prettiest mug mats...just stitch several together for a clever stocking stuffer or last-minute gift!

Frosty Winter Mornings

Blueberry French Toast

Liz Serich
Westland, MI

*For best results, use day-old bread or leave fresh bread slices
on the counter overnight to dry out.*

12 slices bread, crusts trimmed
2 8-oz. pkgs. cream cheese,
   cubed
1 c. blueberries, well drained

12 eggs
2 c. milk
1/3 c. maple syrup

Cut bread into one-inch cubes; place half in a greased 13"x9" baking pan. Arrange cream cheese over bread; top with blueberries and remaining bread. Beat eggs in a large mixing bowl; blend in milk and syrup. Pour mixture over bread; cover and chill 8 hours or overnight. Remove from refrigerator 30 minutes before baking. Bake, covered, at 350 degrees for 30 minutes. Uncover and bake 25 to 30 additional minutes or until golden. Drizzle sauce over top. Serves 8 to 10.

Sauce:

1 c. sugar
2 T. cornstarch
1 c. water

1 c. blueberries
1 T. butter

Combine sugar and cornstarch in a saucepan; add water and bring to a boil over medium heat. Boil for 3 minutes, stirring constantly. Stir in blueberries; reduce heat. Simmer 8 to 10 minutes or until berries burst; stir in butter until melted.

*Wake your family up to Christmas music…what a nice
way to begin the day!*

Frosty Winter Mornings

Sugared Orange Rolls

Kathy Kelley
Libby, MT

Your family will feel like royalty when you serve this!

1 c. sugar
1/2 c. butter
1 T. orange zest

3 7-1/2 oz. tubes refrigerated
   biscuits
Garnish: powdered sugar

Combine sugar and butter in a small saucepan; heat over low heat until butter is melted and sugar is dissolved. Stir in orange zest. Arrange biscuits in a lightly greased Bundt® pan; pour orange mixture over top. Bake at 350 degrees for 20 minutes or until golden. Invert onto a plate and allow to cool. Sprinkle powdered sugar on top. Serves 6 to 8.

Cinnamon-Apple Breakfast Treat

Jennie Swencki
Higley, AZ

A tasty way to use apple pie filling.

3 T. butter
1/2 c. brown sugar, packed
21-oz. can apple pie filling

1-1/2 t. vanilla extract
2 t. cinnamon
12-oz. tube refrigerated biscuits

Melt butter in a saucepan over medium heat; stir in brown sugar, apple pie filling, vanilla and cinnamon. Spread half the mixture in an ungreased 2-quart casserole dish. Cut biscuits into quarters and arrange over top mixture; spoon remaining mixture on top. Bake at 350 degrees for 35 to 40 minutes. Let stand 5 minutes before serving. Serves 4 to 6.

Hot Chocolate Muffins

Carol Hickman
Kingsport, TN

A new breakfast treat for chocolate lovers!

1/2 c. butter, softened
1 c. sugar
4 eggs, separated
6 T. hot chocolate mix
1/2 c. boiling water

2/3 c. milk
3 c. all-purpose flour
6 t. baking powder
1 t. salt
2 t. vanilla extract

Cream butter and sugar together in a large mixing bowl; add egg yolks and beat until well blended. In a separate bowl, dissolve hot chocolate mix in boiling water; add to butter mixture with milk. Sift together flour, baking powder and salt; add to chocolate mixture. Beat egg whites until stiff peaks form; fold egg whites and vanilla into chocolate mixture. Pour batter into greased muffin tins; bake at 375 degrees for 20 to 25 minutes or until centers test done. Makes 1-1/2 to 2 dozen.

For a little nostalgia during breakfast, serve breakfast muffins or biscuits tucked into vintage ornament boxes that have been lined with wax paper.

Frosty Winter Mornings

Buttermilk-Pecan Waffles

Sandy Bernards
Valencia, CA

My family loves these...yours will too!

2 c. all-purpose flour
1 T. baking powder
1 t. baking soda
1/2 t. salt

4 eggs
2 c. buttermilk
1/2 c. butter, melted
3 T. chopped pecans

Sift together first 4 ingredients; set aside. Beat eggs in a mixing bowl until light; mix in buttermilk. Add dry ingredients to egg mixture and beat until smooth. Stir in melted butter. Pour 3/4 cup batter onto a greased and preheated waffle iron; sprinkle with a few pecans. Cook according to manufacturer's directions. Repeat with remaining batter. Makes 7.

'Twas the night before Christmas, when all through the house, Not a creature was stirring, not even a mouse: The stockings were hung by the chimney with care, In hopes that St. Nicholas soon would be there.
-Clement C. Moore

Oven-Baked Maple Pancake

Margo Wright
Bridgeport, NJ

No need for syrup...it's baked right in!

3/4 c. brown sugar, packed
    and divided
1/3 c. butter
1/2 c. maple syrup

1-1/2 c. biscuit baking mix
1 t. cinnamon
1 c. milk
2 eggs

Heat 1/2 cup brown sugar, butter and syrup in a small saucepan over low heat; stir until melted. Pour syrup mixture into a lightly greased 13"x9" baking pan. Combine remaining ingredients and beat with a whisk or fork until well blended; pour over syrup mixture. Bake at 350 degrees for 30 to 35 minutes or until top springs back when touched in the center. Cut into squares; invert onto a serving plate and serve immediately. Serves 6 to 8.

Give a metal cake carrier a holiday look! Spray metal primer on the carrier lid; let dry. Top with two coats of spray paint and allow to dry thoroughly. Use acrylic enamel paints and stencils to add trees, stars, snowmen or holiday greetings. Let dry thoroughly and hand wash only.

Frosty Winter Mornings

Pumpkin-Cream Cheese Spread

Kathy Grashoff
Fort Wayne, IN

Serve with mini bagels for a sweet morning snack.

8-oz. pkg. cream cheese,
   softened
1/2 c. canned pumpkin

1/4 c. sugar
3/4 t. pumpkin pie spice
1/2 t. vanilla extract

Beat all ingredients with an electric mixer on medium speed until smooth. Cover and refrigerate 2 to 3 hours. Makes 1-1/2 cups.

Pecan Mini Muffins

Tisha Brown
Elizabethtown, PA

Just the right size for little fingers to pick up and enjoy!

1 c. brown sugar, packed
1/3 c. all-purpose flour
1/8 t. salt

1 c. chopped pecans
2 eggs
1/2 t. vanilla extract

Mix all ingredients by hand just until moist. Divide dough into mini muffin tins coated with non-stick vegetable spray. Bake at 350 degrees for 20 minutes. Immediately remove muffins from pans and cool on wire racks. Makes 2 dozen.

Stitch a tiny bell onto stockings to jingle whenever children try to sneak a peek!

Sausage-Mozzarella Loaves

Karen Rawson
Elkins, WV

Golden bread loaves filled with cheese and sausage.

2 1-lb. loaves frozen bread
   dough, thawed
1 lb. ground sausage, browned
12-oz. pkg. shredded mozzarella
   cheese

2 eggs, beaten
grated Parmesan cheese to taste

Roll bread loaves into 16"x8" rectangles. Sprinkle sausage and mozzarella cheese over each rectangle. Pour beaten eggs over top. Sprinkle with Parmesan cheese. Roll up each rectangle jelly-roll style, starting at the short end. Place rolls into 2 greased 9"x5" loaf pans. Bake at 400 degrees for 30 to 40 minutes or until tops are golden. Makes 12 to 15 servings.

Tie a greenery swag and bows with long streamers to the stair railing. Pin greeting cards on the streamers so everyone can enjoy them!

Frosty Winter Mornings

Best-Ever Brunch Potatoes

Gaybrielle Ray
Springfield, OH

I created this recipe by just tossing together several of my favorite ingredients...it was a hit! Before brunch was over, it seemed all my guests had asked for the recipe.

2-1/2 lbs. redskin potatoes, diced
3 T. olive oil
8 eggs
1 T. pepper
1 t. salt

8 slices smoked bacon, crisply cooked and crumbled
3/4 c. French onion chip dip
3/4 c. sharp Cheddar cheese
1/2 c. green onions, chopped

Fry potatoes in olive oil in a large skillet until tender. In a separate skillet, scramble eggs until fluffy; add salt and pepper. Fold bacon, chip dip and cheese into the potatoes; stir in scrambled eggs. Turn mixture into a serving dish; sprinkle green onions over top. Serves 6 to 8.

Cut little snowflakes from folded white paper for wintry placecards!

Yuletide Coffee Cake

Joanne Heitzman
Towaco, NJ

This has been a Christmas morning tradition for more than 30 years and it is enjoyed by all. Now my children make this every Christmas for their own morning festivities.

1 c. butter
2 c. sugar
1 t. lemon zest
2 eggs, beaten
1 c. sour cream
2-1/2 t. vanilla extract
1/2 t. lemon extract

2 c. all-purpose flour
1 T. baking powder
1/4 t. salt
1 c. chopped walnuts
4 T. brown sugar, packed
1-1/2 t. cinnamon
Garnish: powdered sugar

Cream butter and sugar together with an electric mixer; blend in lemon zest. Add eggs, sour cream, vanilla and lemon extract; blend well. Sift together flour, baking powder and salt; gradually fold into creamed mixture. Spoon 2/3 batter into a buttered and floured Bundt® pan. In a small bowl, mix together walnuts, brown sugar and cinnamon; sprinkle over batter. Spread remaining batter in pan. Bake at 350 degrees for 55 to 60 minutes. Cool in pan for 10 minutes and invert onto a wire rack; cool 30 minutes before slicing. Sprinkle powdered sugar over top.
Serves 16.

Hang a stocking at the foot of every bed…a fun change from hanging them on the mantel and the kids can dive into them as soon as they wake up!

Christmas Tree Cinnamon Rolls

Paige Lantz
North Little Rock, AR

An edible "tree!"

8-oz. tube refrigerated crescent
   rolls
2 T. margarine, softened
2 T. sugar
1/2 t. cinnamon

2 T. raisins
3/4 c. powdered sugar
1 T. milk
Garnish: red and green candies

Unroll dough into one large rectangle; seal all perforations. Spread margarine evenly over dough. Combine sugar and cinnamon; sprinkle evenly over dough. Sprinkle raisins over sugar and cinnamon. Roll up jelly-roll style, starting from the longest end. Slice roll into 22 pieces. Place slices on a lightly greased baking sheet. Begin with one slice for the top, 2 slices for the second row, 3 for the third row, 4 for the fourth, 5 for the fifth and 6 for the last row. Place remaining slice centered under last row for a tree stem. Bake at 350 degrees for 20 to 25 minutes. Combine powdered sugar and milk; drizzle over warm rolls and decorate with candies. Makes 22 rolls.

Toss quilts on sofas and chairs so they're handy to snuggle up under while everyone opens gifts.

Sausage-Apple Bake

Nichole Clemmer
Harleysville, PA

A hearty breakfast for snowy winter mornings.

1 T. olive oil
1 lb. sausage links, sliced into
   1-1/2 inch pieces
2 onions, chopped

3 apples, cored and chopped
8-oz. pkg. corn muffin mix
1/2 c. sour cream
1 c. shredded Cheddar cheese

Heat oil in a large skillet over medium heat; sauté sausage until brown, about 10 minutes. Add onion and apples; cook until soft and golden, about 5 minutes. Place mixture into a greased 13"x9" baking pan. Prepare corn muffin mix according to package directions; stir sour cream into the batter. Evenly spoon batter on top of filling; sprinkle cheese over top. Bake at 350 degrees for 20 to 25 minutes or until top is golden. Serves 6 to 8.

Colorful tissue paper and a length of raffia create a quick tie up for a gift that's wrapped in a jiffy!

Double Cheese Quiche

Kay Swarthout
Vienna, MO

I like this quick & easy quiche served with grapefruit
and orange sections on the side.

9-inch pie crust
1/2 lb. ground sausage,
   browned
1 c. shredded Cheddar cheese
1 c. shredded Monterey Jack
   cheese

3 eggs, slightly beaten
1/8 t. dry mustard
1/8 t. nutmeg

Line a 9" round baking pan with pie crust. Place cooked sausage in crust; layer cheeses over top. Blend remaining ingredients and pour over cheeses. Bake at 350 degrees for 30 minutes. Let stand 5 minutes before slicing. Serves 6.

Chile-Cheese Puff

Susie Knupp
Somers, MT

Serve with salsa and a dollop of sour cream if you'd like.

5 eggs
1/4 c. all-purpose flour
1/2 t. baking powder
1 c. cottage cheese
8-oz. pkg. shredded Monterey
   Jack cheese

1/4 c. butter, melted
4-1/2 oz. can chopped green
   chiles, drained

Beat eggs in a large mixing bowl; stir in next 5 ingredients. Fold in green chiles. Pour mixture into a greased 8"x8" baking pan. Bake at 350 degrees for 40 to 45 minutes or until center tests done. Serves 4.

Pumpkin Cream Muffins

Cheri Emery
Quincy, IL

*Sweet muffins with a delicious cream cheese center. For a welcome
holiday surprise, deliver a batch of these to neighbors
on a chilly winter morning.*

3 eggs, divided
1-1/3 c. sugar, divided
1-1/4 c. all-purpose flour
2 t. cinnamon
3/4 c. oil

1 c. canned pumpkin
1 t. baking soda
1/2 t. salt
8-oz. pkg. cream cheese,
softened

Combine 2 eggs, one cup sugar, flour, cinnamon, oil, pumpkin, baking
soda and salt; set aside. In a separate bowl, blend together cream
cheese, remaining egg and sugar. Pour pumpkin mixture into greased
muffin tins, filling 2/3 full. Place a heaping teaspoon of cream filling in
the center of each muffin. Sprinkle with one teaspoon topping mixture.
Bake at 350 degrees for 15 to 18 minutes. Makes 1-1/2 dozen.

Topping:

1/4 c. sugar
1/4 t. cinnamon

3 T. all-purpose flour
2 T. butter

Combine all ingredients until crumbly.

A retro green breadbox makes a nice tree stand for a
small kitchen tree. Don't forget to pour in a little pea
gravel around the tree base to keep it from leaning.

Frosty Winter Mornings

Blueberry-Sour Cream Breakfast Cake
LaVerne Fang
Joliet, IL

Brown sugar, cinnamon and nuts swirled with blueberries...yummy!

1 c. butter	2 c. cake flour
2 c. sugar	1/4 t. salt
2 eggs	1 t. baking powder
1 c. sour cream	1/2 c. blueberries, well drained
1/2 t. vanilla extract	Garnish: powdered sugar

Cream butter and sugar; add eggs. Fold in sour cream and vanilla. Sift together dry ingredients and add to mixture. Fold in blueberries. Pour 1/3 batter into a greased and floured Bundt® pan; sprinkle with half the filling. Pour 1/3 batter over top; sprinkle with remaining filling. Top with remaining batter. Gently swirl cake with a spatula. Bake at 350 degrees for one hour. Cool and invert onto a serving platter. Dust with powdered sugar. Serves 12 to 16.

Filling:

1/2 c. brown sugar, packed	1/2 c. chopped nuts
1 t. cinnamon	

Mix until combined.

Add a frosty look to window panes by snipping snowflakes from a roll of wax paper. Attach them with a drop of rubber cement; it rubs right off when you take the snowflakes down.

Santa's Raisin Scones

Donna Reid
Payson, AZ

When my sons were younger, they liked to help make these treats. We always left some out for Santa and his reindeer on Christmas Eve.

1-3/4 c. all-purpose flour
1/3 c. sugar
1 t. baking powder
1/2 t. baking soda
2/3 c. buttermilk
1/3 c. butter, melted

1/3 c. raisins
1 c. powdered sugar
1/2 t. vanilla extract
1 to 2 T. water
Garnish: colorful sprinkles

Combine first 4 ingredients; stir in buttermilk, butter and raisins until just moistened. Spoon dough into 6 to 8 equal mounds on a greased baking sheet. Bake at 400 degrees for 18 to 20 minutes or until golden; cool. Combine powdered sugar, vanilla and water; drizzle over scones. Decorate with colorful sprinkles. Serves 6 to 8.

For a personalized gift tag, string fresh cranberries on wire and shape it into an initial!

Frosty Winter Mornings

Sugary Pumpkin Doughnuts

Paula Vento
Pasadena, CA

The dough is prepared the night before, so making these tasty old-fashioned doughnuts is a breeze.

3-1/2 c. all-purpose flour
1 T. baking powder
1 t. baking soda
1 t. salt
1/2 t. cinnamon
1/2 t. ground ginger
1/4 c. butter, softened

1-1/4 c. sugar, divided
2 eggs
2/3 c. canned pumpkin
2/3 c. buttermilk
1/2 c. brown sugar, packed
oil for deep frying

Sift together the first 6 ingredients. Cream butter and 3/4 cup sugar with an electric mixer in a large bowl. Add eggs, one at a time, beating well after each addition. Beat in 1/4 cup flour mixture; add pumpkin and buttermilk. Add remaining flour mixture, stirring until just blended. Cover and refrigerate 3 hours or overnight. Combine remaining sugar and brown sugar in a plastic bag; set aside. Roll dough to 1/3-inch thickness. Cut into doughnuts; transfer to a floured surface and let stand 10 minutes. Heat 1/2-inch oil in a large skillet; cook doughnuts on both sides until golden and cooked through, about 5 minutes. Place on paper towels to drain. While still warm, place each doughnut in the bag with sugar and shake to coat. Makes 2 to 3 dozen.

Wrap a few snowballs in aluminum foil and pack them away in the freezer. Bring them out at the Fourth of July party (when the weather's really hot) and have a summer snowball toss!

Fruit-Filled Breakfast Cups

Marcia Smith
Portage, MI

Every Christmas Eve afternoon, my family travels around our neighborhood delivering Christmas morning breakfast to our friends, neighbors and family. We include these fruit cups, homemade muffins and flavored butter.

2 10-oz. pkgs. frozen sliced
   strawberries, thawed
2 6-oz. cans frozen orange juice
   concentrate, thawed
2 20-oz. cans crushed
   pineapple

16-oz. can mandarin oranges
1/3 c. lemon juice
6 bananas, sliced

Without draining fruit, combine strawberries, orange juice, pineapple, oranges, lemon juice and bananas in a large bowl; mix well. Spoon mixture into 5-ounce plastic serving cups. Freeze until firm; package in plastic airtight bags if needed. Remove from freezer 30 minutes before serving. Makes about one dozen.

Shop flea markets for all kinds of cookie cutters...they
make terrific ornaments, package
tie-on's and napkin rings.

Frosty Winter Mornings

Baked Brown Sugar French Toast

Deborah Byrne
Clinton, CT

Slice into French toast sticks…easy for little ones to hold.

2/3 c. brown sugar, packed
1/2 c. butter, melted
2 t. cinnamon
6 eggs

1-3/4 c. milk
1-lb. loaf French bread, cut into
    one-inch slices
Garnish: powdered sugar

Combine brown sugar, butter and cinnamon; spread evenly in a greased 15"x10" baking pan. Set aside. Combine eggs and milk in a shallow dish. Place bread in dish and soak for 5 minutes, turning once. Place bread over sugar mixture. Bake at 350 degrees for 25 to 30 minutes or until golden. Serve sugar-side up. Dust with powdered sugar. Serves 4 to 6.

Quick Jam Turnovers

Jennifer Dutcher
Gooseberry Patch

I came up with this treat the first Christmas morning my husband and I spent together. He likes grape and I like strawberry, so I made both kinds!

12-oz. tube refrigerated biscuits
3/4 c. strawberry or grape jam

2 T. milk
sugar

Flatten each biscuit with a fork to twice its original size on an ungreased baking sheet. Place a tablespoon of jam in the center of each biscuit. Fold over each biscuit and seal edges with a fork. Brush tops with milk and sprinkle with sugar. Bake at 375 degrees for 12 to 15 minutes. Makes one dozen.

Christmas Apple Rolls

Karen Hess
Scott City, KS

This is our traditional family Christmas breakfast. I received this recipe as a part of a wedding gift, 20 years ago, from my mother-in-law. However because she makes enough for the whole family, I've never had to prepare it!

1 c. milk	1 pkg. active dry yeast
4 c. all-purpose flour	1/4 c. warm water
1/4 c. sugar	2 eggs, beaten
1 t. salt	1 c. powdered sugar
1 t. lemon zest	1 to 2 T. water
1 c. shortening	

Scald milk, then cool to lukewarm. In a large bowl, combine flour, sugar, salt and lemon zest. Cut in shortening to resemble coarse crumbs. In a separate bowl, dissolve yeast in warm water and add to flour mixture along with eggs and warm milk. Lightly combine. Cover dough and refrigerate overnight. Remove cover and divide dough in half. On a floured surface, roll one half into a 18"x15" rectangle; spread with half the filling. Fold in both long sides to form 3 layers. Repeat with remaining portion of dough. Cut both rolls into one-inch strips. Hold ends of strips and twist, then shape into candy canes. Arrange rolls on lightly greased baking sheets. Bake at 400 degrees for 10 to 15 minutes. Combine powdered sugar and water; drizzle over rolls. Makes 30.

Filling:

1-1/2 c. apples, cored, peeled and finely chopped	1/3 c. sugar
3/4 c. chopped pecans	2 t. cinnamon

Combine all ingredients and mix well.

Cranberry Wreaths

Michelle Camp
Peoria, IL

Drizzled with icing, these wreaths are almost too pretty to eat, but too delicious not to!

3 c. all-purpose flour, divided
1/4 c. sugar
1 pkg. instant yeast
1 t. salt
3/4 c. evaporated milk
1/4 c. water

1/4 c. butter
2 eggs
1 c. cranberries, chopped
1/2 c. sugar
1-1/2 t. orange zest

Combine 2 cups flour, sugar, yeast and salt in a large bowl. Heat milk, water and butter in a saucepan until hot to the touch; gradually stir into dry ingredients. Mix in room-temperature eggs and enough remaining flour to make a stiff batter. Cover loosely with plastic wrap; refrigerate 2 hours or overnight. Combine cranberries, sugar and orange zest in a small saucepan; bring to a boil over medium heat. Cook and stir for 5 minutes; cool. Punch down chilled dough. Turn out on a lightly floured surface and roll to a 21"x12" rectangle; spread cranberry filling over dough. Fold short ends toward the middle, overlapping to form a 12"x7" rectangle; cut into twelve, one-inch strips. Holding ends of each strip, twist in opposite directions 3 times. Bring ends of each twist together to form wreaths; place on greased baking sheets. Cover and let rise in a warm place until almost double in bulk. Bake at 350 degrees for 25 minutes; cool on wire rack. Drizzle icing over top. Makes one dozen.

Powdered Sugar Icing:

1 c. powdered sugar
4 to 5 t. evaporated milk

1/2 t. vanilla extract

Combine all ingredients, beating until smooth.

Casserole
Vickie

...akfast at our house all winter long.

...croutons
1 c. shredded Cheddar cheese
4 eggs
2 c. milk

1/2 t. hot pepper sauce
1/8 t. pepper
4 to 5 slices bacon, crisply
    cooked and crumbled

Combine croutons and cheese in a 2-quart casserole dish coated with non-stick vegetable spray. In a mixing bowl, beat eggs with milk, hot pepper sauce and pepper; pour over croutons and cheese. Sprinkle bacon over top. Bake at 350 degrees for 45 minutes. Serves 4 to 6.

Christmas Morn Omelet
Marcy Klos
Cortland, NY

I make this dish ahead of time and just pop it in the oven Christmas morning so I can watch the kids open their gifts.

12 slices bread, divided
6 slices cooked ham
6 slices American cheese
8 eggs
3 c. milk

1 t. dry mustard
1 t. salt
1/2 c. butter, melted
1 c. corn flake cereal, crushed

Line a greased 13"x9" baking pan with 6 slices of bread; layer ham and cheese on top. Arrange remaining bread slices over cheese. Combine eggs, milk, mustard and salt in a mixing bowl; beat well. Pour mixture over bread. Cover and refrigerate overnight. Mix together butter and corn flake cereal; spread on top of omelet. Bake at 350 degrees for 45 minutes. Makes 6 to 8 servings.

Frosty Winter Mornings

Holiday Ham Soufflé

Allison James Santoiemma
Grinnell, IA

Christmas at my parents' house is quite an occasion...we're all thrilled to be together as a family again. This yummy recipe was handed down from my Grandma Graves to my mother, and while the kids look forward to the gifts, the adults look forward to this!

16 slices bread, crusts trimmed
   and divided
4 c. cooked ham, diced and
   divided
2 8-oz. pkgs. shredded Swiss
   cheese, divided
2 8-oz. pkgs. shredded Cheddar
   cheese, divided

3 c. milk
6 eggs
1/2 t. onion powder
1/2 t. dry mustard
3 c. corn flake cereal, crushed
1/2 c. butter, melted

Layer 8 bread slices on the bottom of a lightly greased 13"x9" baking pan. Top with 2 cups ham, one package Swiss cheese and one package Cheddar cheese; repeat layers with remaining bread, ham and cheeses. Combine milk, eggs, onion powder and dry mustard; pour over layers. Cover pan and refrigerate overnight; remove 30 minutes before baking and uncover. Combine corn flake cereal and butter; sprinkle over layers. Bake at 375 degrees for one hour; let stand 15 minutes before slicing. Serves 6 to 8.

Family coming for a holiday brunch? Copy one of Grandma's tried & true recipes onto a festive card, then punch a hole in the corner and tie the card to a napkin with a length of ribbon...a sweet keepsake.

Chocolatey Banana Muffins
Kimberly Johnston-Orazio
Derry, PA

Why leave out cookies? Santa would love these!

2 c. all-purpose flour
1 c. sugar
1 T. baking powder
1/2 t. salt
1 c. bananas, mashed

1/3 c. milk
1/3 c. creamy peanut butter
3 T. oil
1 egg
1 c. chocolate chips

Combine flour, sugar, baking powder and salt in a mixing bowl. Add bananas, milk, peanut butter, oil and egg; stir until dry ingredients are moistened. Fold in chocolate chips. Spoon batter into muffin tins coated with non-stick vegetable spray. Bake at 350 degrees for 25 to 30 minutes or until centers test done. Makes one dozen.

Cinnamon Toast Cut-Outs
Lisa Johnson
Hallsville, TX

Kids big and little love cinnamon toast!

3 to 4 bread slices
butter

1 T. cinnamon
2 T. sugar

Cut bread slices with cookie cutters; spread butter on top and toast until golden. Mix together cinnamon and sugar; sprinkle over warm bread. Serves 2.

Frosty Winter Mornings

Cheery Cherry Muffins

Robin Lutz
Cranberry Township, PA

The chocolate chips make these muffins extra-special!

2 c. all-purpose flour
1/2 c. sugar
1/2 c. brown sugar, packed
2 t. baking powder
1/2 t. baking soda
1/2 t. salt

2 c. chocolate chips, divided
1/2 c. candied cherries, chopped
1/2 c. milk
1/3 c. oil
1 egg

Combine first 6 ingredients in a large bowl; stir in one cup chocolate chips and cherries. Set aside. In a separate bowl, combine milk, oil and egg; stir into flour mixture until just moistened. Spoon batter into paper-lined muffin tins until full. Sprinkle remaining chocolate chips over tops. Bake at 375 degrees for 18 to 21 minutes. Makes one dozen.

A fun countdown to Christmas! Get the family together during breakfast and think up 25 fun holiday activities like making gingerbread cookies for classmates, dancing to holiday music, sledding or reading a Christmas story. Write each on a paper strip, link them together and then pull one off each day in December and do the activity together.

Ham & Cheddar Hashbrown Bake

Jo Ann

A tasty, easy-to-make breakfast I know I can count on.

3 c. frozen shredded
　　hashbrowns, thawed
1/3 c. butter, melted
1 c. cooked ham, diced
1 c. shredded Cheddar cheese

1/4 c. green pepper, chopped
2 eggs
1/2 c. milk
salt and pepper to taste

Press hashbrowns between paper towels to remove excess moisture.
Press into the bottom and up the sides of an ungreased 9" round
baking pan; drizzle with butter. Bake at 425 degrees for 25 minutes.
Combine ham, cheese and green pepper; spoon over baked crust. In a
small bowl, beat eggs, milk, salt and pepper; pour over ham mixture.
Bake at 350 degrees for 25 to 30 minutes or until center tests done.
Let stand 10 minutes before slicing. Makes 6 servings.

Freeze tiny candy canes
along with orange juice
in ice cube trays...a
tasty and clever way to
keep breakfast juice
from becoming diluted.

Family & Friends Together

Parmesan-Artichoke Chicken

Cynthia Madsen
Brooklyn Park, MN

*This recipe turns a favorite appetizer into
a quick & easy main dish.*

14-oz. can artichoke hearts,
    drained and chopped
3/4 c. grated Parmesan cheese
3/4 c. mayonnaise

1/8 t. garlic powder
4 boneless, skinless chicken
    breasts

Combine artichokes, cheese, mayonnaise and garlic powder in a
mixing bowl. Place chicken in a greased 11"x7" baking pan; spread
artichoke mixture over top. Bake at 375 degrees for 30 to 35 minutes
or until chicken juices run clear when pierced with a fork. Serves 4.

Invite friends to a holiday dinner with memorable
invitations. First, use a rubber stamp to make an
all-over pattern on heavy cardstock. Then print the
invitation on sheets of vellum and secure them to the
cardstock with old-fashioned photo corners.

Chicken-Stuffed Shells

Kathleen Kosinski
West Mifflin, PA

If you're looking for a special dish for company, try this one…it's oh-so simple and absolutely delicious!

30 to 36 jumbo shells
6-oz. pkg. herb-flavored
   stuffing mix
2 c. chicken, cooked and diced

1 c. mayonnaise
2 10-3/4 oz. cans cream of
   chicken soup
grated Parmesan cheese to taste

Cook shells in boiling water according to package directions. Prepare stuffing mix according to package directions; stir in chicken and mayonnaise. In a separate bowl, mix soup with one soup can water; pour half on the bottom of a lightly greased 13"x9" baking pan. Stuff shells with stuffing mixture; place shells open-side up in pan. Pour remaining soup mixture over top. Sprinkle with cheese. Cover and bake at 350 degrees for 45 to 60 minutes. Serves 8 to 10.

Set a sleigh, wagon or toboggan filled with greenery, apples and pine cones on the porch…what a cheery way to greet family & friends!

Mushroom & Herb Stuffed Meatballs

Ann Harris
Alberta, Canada

These meatballs are a family favorite when the weather turns chilly.

3 lbs. ground beef
1 egg
salt and pepper to taste
3 c. bread crumbs
1 onion, chopped
1/2 c. carrot, grated
4-oz. can sliced mushrooms,
    drained

2 T. dried sage
2 T. dried thyme
1/4 c. butter, melted
10-3/4 oz. can golden
    mushroom soup
1/2 c. catsup

Mix together beef, egg, salt and pepper; divide into 12 equal parts, form into patties and set aside. In a mixing bowl, combine bread crumbs, onion, carrot, mushrooms, sage, thyme and butter; add enough water to make a moist stuffing. Divide stuffing into 12 equal parts; form each into a 1-1/2 to 2-inch ball. Place a stuffing ball on each patty; shape patty around stuffing until it is completely covered and seams are smooth. Place meatballs in an ungreased 13"x9" baking pan. Combine soup and catsup; pour over meatballs. Bake at 375 degrees for one hour and 15 minutes or until tops begin to open. Serves 6 to 8.

Wrapping a gift for a music lover? Use copies of sheet music as wrapping paper...how clever!

Sesame Shrimp & Pasta

Jennifer Breeden
Mobile, AL

This dish is easy to prepare and looks so elegant when served.

2 T. soy sauce
1 T. sesame oil
2 t. lemon juice
1 t. garlic powder
1/8 t. lemon-pepper seasoning
1 lb. shrimp, peeled and
    deveined

1 T. sesame seed
16-oz. pkg. angel hair pasta,
    cooked
16-oz. jar alfredo sauce, warmed

Mix together first 5 ingredients to make a marinade; add shrimp and refrigerate for 30 minutes. Lightly spray a 10" skillet with non-stick vegetable spray; pour shrimp with marinade into skillet and sprinkle sesame seed over top. Sauté shrimp just until opaque and pink. Spoon cooked pasta on the center of 8 dinner plates; top each with warmed alfredo sauce. Spoon a portion of the shrimp and marinade over pasta and sauce. Serves 8.

Nestle a pair of woolly mittens and lots of greenery in a round antique sifter for a new spin on a front door Christmas wreath!

Cheesy Ham & Corn Chowder

Carol Burns
Gooseberry Patch

Hearty soups like this are filling enough to be a meal and the aroma gives a "welcome home" feeling when family & friends come to visit.

1 T. butter
1/2 c. onion, chopped
2 T. all-purpose flour
1/2 c. green pepper, chopped
14-1/2 oz. can chicken broth
4 new red potatoes, sliced
1/2 t. dried sage

1/4 t. pepper
1/2 lb. cooked ham, cubed
1-1/2 c. milk
10-oz. pkg. frozen corn
8-oz. pkg. pasteurized process
   cheese spread, cubed

Melt butter in a large saucepan; stir in onion and cook over medium heat until tender. Stir in flour until blended. Add green pepper, chicken broth, potatoes, sage and pepper; stir to blend. Cover and cook until potatoes are tender, about 15 to 20 minutes. Add remaining ingredients; cook and stir until heated through, about 8 to 10 minutes. Serves 4 to 6.

Fill a glass punch bowl with cranberries and floating candles for an easy, but elegant centerpiece!

Bacon, Mushroom & Zucchini Frittata
Kathy Schroeder
Riverside, CA

After an afternoon of holiday shopping, this meal is an all-time favorite.

2 T. butter, divided
1/2 lb. zucchini, sliced
1 red onion, chopped
1/2 c. sun-dried tomatoes, chopped
1/2 lb. sliced mushrooms
2 cloves garlic, chopped

1 t. dried parsley
6 eggs, beaten
1 lb. bacon, crisply cooked and crumbled
1/2 c. shredded Swiss cheese
salt and pepper to taste

Melt one tablespoon butter in a large skillet over medium heat; add zucchini and onion. Cook until vegetables begin to soften. Add sun-dried tomatoes, mushrooms, garlic and parsley; sauté for one minute. Place eggs in a mixing bowl; add bacon, zucchini mixture and Swiss cheese. Season with salt and pepper. Heat remaining butter in skillet over medium heat. Pour egg mixture into skillet; reduce heat to low and shake skillet to level all ingredients. Cook until eggs are set, about 10 minutes. Invert on a large plate, then slide back into skillet, cooked-side up. Return to medium heat and cook until golden, about 5 minutes. Serves 4 to 6.

An old wooden cheese box makes a one-of-a-kind candle holder.
Filled with sand, lots of votives can be nestled inside to give off a warm holiday glow.

Italian Spaghetti Pie

*Sue Webber
Kent, WA*

My sons' most requested dish any time of year!

3 c. prepared spaghetti
2 T. butter
1/3 c. grated Parmesan cheese
2 eggs, beaten
1 c. cottage cheese
1 lb. ground beef
1/2 c. onion, chopped
1/4 c. green pepper, chopped

8-oz. can chopped tomatoes
6-oz. can tomato paste
1 t. sugar
1 t. dried oregano, crushed
1/2 t. garlic salt
1/2 c. shredded mozzarella
cheese

Place cooked spaghetti in a mixing bowl; stir in butter until melted.
Add Parmesan cheese and eggs. Pour mixture into a buttered
10" round baking pan. Spread cottage cheese over spaghetti. Cook
ground beef, onion and green pepper until beef is browned and
vegetables are tender; drain. Stir in undrained tomatoes, tomato paste,
sugar, oregano and garlic salt; heat through. Pour beef mixture over
cottage cheese. Bake at 350 degrees for 20 minutes. Sprinkle
mozzarella cheese over top; bake 5 additional minutes or until cheese
melts. Serves 6.

*Quick tip...bobby
pins are a handy way
to secure twinkling
lights to a garland!*

Creamy Chicken Tettrazini

Shannon Anderson
Concord, NC

A topping of croutons gives this delicious crunch!

2 10-3/4 oz. cans Cheddar
    cheese soup
1-1/2 c. milk
2 cubes chicken bouillon
12-oz. pkg. wide egg noodles,
    cooked
1 onion, chopped

3 c. chicken, cooked and diced
1-1/2 c. sourdough-cheese
    croutons, crushed
3 T. butter, melted
3-1/2 c. shredded Monterey Jack
    cheese

Combine soup, milk and bouillon cubes in a saucepan; cook over medium heat until warmed through. In a large bowl, combine noodles, onion, chicken and soup mixture; stir to combine. Place mixture in a greased 13"x9" baking pan. Toss croutons with melted butter in a small bowl. Sprinkle cheese over noodles and top with croutons. Bake at 350 degrees for 40 to 50 minutes or until golden. Serves 6 to 8.

Set green votives inside jelly jars that are half full of tiny white pebbles...march them right up the walkway for a lighted path guests will love!

Cranberry-Glazed Ham

Beverly Smith
Malin, OR

*Serve slices topped with a generous spoonful of the
brown sugar-cranberry glaze...wonderful!*

5 to 6-lb. ham
16-oz. can jellied
   cranberry sauce
1 c. brown sugar, packed

1/4 c. orange juice
1/2 t. ground cloves
1/4 t. cinnamon
1/4 t. allspice

Bake ham at 350 degrees for 18 to 20 minutes per pound or until
meat thermometer registers 160 degrees. While ham is baking,
combine remaining ingredients in a saucepan; heat slowly, whisking
until smooth. Spoon half the glaze mixture over the ham 30 minutes
before removing it from the oven; continue baking for 30 minutes.
Serve with remaining glaze. Serves 8 to 10.

Tangy Beef Brisket

Angela Blevins
Louisville, KY

*This is a favorite family recipe that is requested at
just about every holiday.*

3 to 4-lb. brisket, trimmed
8-oz. bottle Catalina dressing

12-oz. bottle chili sauce

Place brisket in a large baking pan. Mix together dressing and chili
sauce; pour over beef. Cover and bake at 350 degrees for 2-1/2 to
3 hours. Serves 4 to 6.

*May happiness be guided to your house
by the candle of Christmas.*
-Old Blessing

♡ Family & Friends Together ❄

Turkey & Broccoli Casserole

Judy Davis
Muskogee, OK

This is a cinch to make for an office party or church social.

6-oz. pkg. turkey-flavored
  stuffing mix
6-oz. can French-fried onion
  rings, divided
10-oz. bag frozen chopped
  broccoli, thawed

1-1/4 oz. pkg. nacho cheese
  sauce mix
1 c. sour cream
1 bunch green onions, chopped
2 c. turkey, cooked and chopped

Prepare stuffing mix according to package directions; spread in a greased 13"x9" baking pan. Sprinkle half the onion rings over top; arrange broccoli over onions. Prepare cheese sauce according to package directions; stir in sour cream. Fold in green onions and turkey. Pour mixture over broccoli. Bake at 350 degrees for 35 to 45 minutes; sprinkle remaining onions over top during the last 15 minutes. Serves 6 to 8.

Expand a collection of holiday dishes…swap with friends! Invite everyone to bring two serving dishes, glasses or bowls to a mix-and-match party to trade. Everyone goes home with something new.

Sweet-Tart Chicken

Jo Ann

*Orange marmalade and cranberry sauce gives this
ready-in-a-flash dinner it's sweet-tart taste.*

1/2 c. chili sauce
1/2 c. cranberry sauce
2 T. orange marmalade
1/8 t. allspice

1/8 t. ground cloves
4 to 6 boneless, skinless
   chicken breasts
2 t. oil

Combine first 5 ingredients in a mixing bowl; set aside. In a large
skillet, slowly brown chicken on both sides in oil. Pour prepared sauce
over chicken. Simmer 8 to 10 minutes or until chicken is cooked
through, turning and basting occasionally. Serves 4 to 6.

Traditional Pork & Sauerkraut

*Laura deMattei
New Fairfield, CT*

*Don't forget the good things that go with this...mashed potatoes
topped with gravy and buttery dinner rolls.*

16-oz. can sauerkraut, drained
1 onion, chopped
16-oz. can whole tomatoes

3 lbs. pork ribs
3/4 c. brown sugar, packed

Spread sauerkraut in an ungreased 13"x9" baking pan. Layer onion,
tomatoes and ribs on top. Sprinkle sugar over ribs. Cover and bake
at 325 degrees for 2 hours and 15 minutes. Uncover and bake
45 additional minutes or until meat is tender. Serves 4 to 6.

Zesty Onion Meat Loaf

Lara Shore
Independence, MO

Great for dinner and ready the next day for quick sandwiches.

1-1/2 lbs. ground beef
11-1/8 oz. can Italian tomato
  soup, divided
1-1/3 c. French-fried onion
  rings, divided

2 T. Worcestershire sauce
3/4 t. salt
1/4 t. pepper
1 egg

Combine beef, 1/3 cup soup, 2/3 cup onion rings, Worcestershire sauce, salt, pepper and egg. Place mixture in an ungreased 8"x4" loaf pan and form into a loaf, sealing cracks and seams. Bake at 350 degrees for one hour; drain off fat. Spoon remaining soup over loaf; top with remaining onion rings. Return loaf to oven for 5 additional minutes. Serves 4 to 6.

Pile sparkly, nostalgic fruit ornaments into a compote bowl or on a cake stand...terrific on a sideboard!

Cheese & Mushroom-Stuffed Chicken *Katherine Guell*
Fond du Lac, WI

Boneless chicken goes from simple to supreme in this recipe!

3 to 4 lbs. boneless, skinless
    chicken breasts
5 T. butter, divided
4-oz. can sliced mushrooms
1/4 c. onion, chopped
1/4 t. garlic powder

2 c. shredded Cheddar cheese,
    divided
1 c. shredded mozzarella cheese,
    divided
1/4 t. lemon pepper
1/3 c. seasoned bread crumbs

Flatten chicken breasts between wax paper; set aside. Melt one
tablespoon butter over medium heat in a skillet. Add mushrooms,
onion and garlic powder; cook until vegetables are tender, about
7 minutes. Remove from heat and cool slightly. Stir in 1/2 cup
Cheddar cheese and 1/2 cup mozzarella cheese; spread mixture onto
each chicken breast. Roll up each chicken breast and secure with
toothpicks. Melt 2 tablespoons butter in a small bowl; dip chicken into
butter then into bread crumbs. Place chicken on lightly greased baking
sheets. Drizzle with remaining butter. Sprinkle with remaining cheeses.
Bake at 450 degrees for 18 to 20 minutes. Serves 6 to 8.

Fill a metal tub with sand and tuck lots of dripless
tapers inside. Set it in the fireplace opening where it
can cast a soft glow.

White Chili

Maureen Viggiani
North Chili, NY

*You can also make this early and heat in a
slow cooker on low all day.*

1 T. olive oil
1 lb. boneless, skinless chicken
   breasts, cubed
1/4 c. onion, chopped
1 c. chicken broth
4-1/2 oz. can chopped green
   chiles
1 t. garlic powder

1 t. cumin
1/2 t. dried oregano
1/2 t. cilantro
1/8 t. ground red pepper
19-oz. can cannellini beans
Garnish: shredded Monterey
   Jack cheese

Heat oil in a large saucepan over high heat; add chicken and cook
4 to 5 minutes, stirring often. Remove chicken with a slotted spoon.
Add onion to pan; sauté 2 minutes. Stir in broth, green chiles and
spices; simmer 2 minutes. Add chicken and beans; simmer
5 additional minutes. Garnish with cheese before serving. Serves 4.

The prettiest party
favors…combine powdered
sugar and enough water to
make a stiff frosting. Brush
frosting onto apples in
snowflake patterns. Let
the frosting harden. For
extra sparkle, sprinkle
granulated sugar or
edible glitter on before the
frosting dries.

Taco Salad Bake

Kelly Laughery
New Windsor, MD

A terrific family dinner after a day spent trimming the tree.

1-1/2 lbs. ground beef
1-1/4 oz. pkg. taco seasoning
  mix
3/4 c. water
1 c. mayonnaise
16-oz. jar salsa, divided
13-1/2 oz. pkg. white corn
  tortilla chips, crushed and
  divided

8-oz. pkg. shredded Cheddar
  cheese, divided
8-oz. pkg. shredded mozzarella
  cheese, divided
3 c. salad mix
1 tomato, chopped
1 bunch green onions, chopped
4-oz. can sliced black olives

Brown beef in a skillet; drain and add taco seasoning and water. Stir in mayonnaise and 1/2 jar salsa; blend well. Reserve one cup mixture; place remaining mixture in the bottom of an ungreased 13"x9" baking pan. Reserve one cup chips and layer remaining chips over beef mixture; top with one cup Cheddar and one cup mozzarella cheese. Layer salad mix, tomato, green onions and olives over top. Sprinkle remaining cheese over all; top with reserved chips and beef mixture. Bake at 350 degrees for 10 to 15 minutes or until cheese is melted. Serves 5 to 6.

Write the lyrics to a favorite
Christmas carol on a solid
color teacup and saucer
using glass paint…a simple,
one-of-a-kind gift!

Enchiladas Fantastica

Debbie Hammer
Chico, TX

Warm up to this hearty dinner after an afternoon spent playing in the snow...it bakes in only 22 minutes!

1 lb. ground beef, browned
2 c. picante sauce, divided
10-oz. pkg. frozen chopped
   broccoli, thawed
2 T. cumin, divided
1/2 t. salt
8-oz. pkg. cream cheese, cubed

12 8-inch flour tortillas,
   warmed
14-1/2 oz. can diced tomatoes
1 c. shredded Cheddar cheese
Garnish: shredded lettuce, olive
   slices and sour cream

Combine beef, one cup picante sauce, broccoli, 1-1/2 teaspoons cumin and salt in a large skillet; cook until most liquid has evaporated. Stir in cream cheese until melted. Spoon 1/3 cup filling down the center of each tortilla. Roll up each tortilla and place seam-side down in a lightly greased 13"x9" baking pan. Combine tomatoes, remaining picante sauce and cumin; spoon over enchiladas. Bake at 350 degrees for 20 minutes. Sprinkle with Cheddar cheese; return to oven for 2 additional minutes. Garnish with lettuce, olives and sour cream. Serves 6.

Make a sweet treat wreath by inserting toothpicks into red and white gumdrops, then pushing the toothpicks securely into a foam wreath.

Spinach Lasagna

Arundi Venkayya Cox
Dayton, OH

*This is one of my favorite recipes to make during the holidays.
It's quick & easy and most people don't believe it's vegetarian!*

1 onion, chopped
2 cloves garlic
3 t. olive oil
10-oz. pkg. frozen chopped
   spinach, thawed and drained
1/4 t. dried rosemary
1/4 t. dried oregano
1/4 t. dried basil
8-oz. container ricotta cheese
1/2 c. grated Parmesan cheese
16-oz. pkg. shredded mozzarella
   cheese, divided

26-oz. jar spaghetti sauce,
   divided
12 T. water, divided
16-oz. pkg. no-boil lasagna
   noodles, divided
12-oz. pkg. vegetarian Italian
   sausage, divided
Garnish: grated Parmesan
   cheese

Sauté onion and garlic in oil until tender. Add spinach, rosemary,
oregano and basil; cook 2 to 3 minutes. In a large mixing bowl,
combine ricotta cheese, Parmesan cheese and half the mozzarella
cheese. Add spinach and onion mixture; mix well. Spoon 1/3 spaghetti
sauce in the bottom of a 13"x9" baking pan coated with non-stick
vegetable spray. Add 6 tablespoons water. Layer 1/3 lasagna noodles,
1/3 spinach mixture, 1/3 sausage and 1/3 spaghetti sauce; add
remaining 6 tablespoons water. Repeat layering noodles, spinach
mixture and sausage 2 times. Pour remaining sauce on top; sprinkle
remaining mozzarella cheese over all. Bake at 400 degrees for 35 to
40 minutes. Sprinkle with Parmesan cheese. Serves 6 to 8.

*Dress up a mantel with a cranberry swag...just string
fresh cranberries on lengths of wax thread.*

Best-Ever Chicken Casserole

A down-home dish that's always requested by family & friends.

4 boneless, skinless chicken breasts
salt and pepper to taste
2 c. shredded Swiss cheese

2 10-3/4 oz. cans cream of chicken soup
2 c. herb-flavored stuffing mix
3/4 c. butter

Place chicken in a large stockpot; cover with water and salt and pepper to taste. Bring to a boil, cooking until chicken is done, about 20 to 25 minutes. Drain and let cool. Cut chicken into bite-size pieces; arrange on the bottom of a lightly greased 13"x9" baking pan. Sprinkle Swiss cheese over chicken and spread cream of chicken soup over cheese. Sprinkle stuffing mix over soup; drizzle butter over top. Bake at 325 degrees for 30 minutes. Serves 6 to 8.

Cover buttons with festive fabric, then glue to ribbons; let glue dry. Tie around napkins for the easiest napkin rings!

Hearty Vegetable-Beef Stew

Laurie Park
Columbus, OH

*Passed from friend to friend, this will find a
permanent home in your recipe file.*

14-1/2 oz. can diced tomatoes
1 c. water
3 T. quick-cooking tapioca
2 t. sugar
1 t. salt
1/2 t. pepper

2 lbs. stew meat, cubed
4 carrots, sliced
3 potatoes, peeled and quartered
2 stalks celery, sliced
1 onion, chopped
1 slice bread, cubed

Combine the first 6 ingredients in a large bowl; mix well. Stir in
remaining ingredients. Pour mixture into a greased 3-quart casserole
dish; cover and bake at 375 degrees for 1-1/2 to 2 hours or until meat
and vegetables are tender. Serves 6 to 8.

Put a spin on a
ribbon memory
board and arrange
the ribbons into a
snowflake design!
What a great way to
keep track of
holiday party
invitations, cards
and photos.

Chicken-Pasta Bake

Helene Brown
Kalispell, MT

*The variety of ingredients give this basic chicken
casserole a very special flavor.*

3/4 c. grated Parmesan cheese,
  divided
2 c. chicken, cooked and cubed
1/2 c. cooked ham, diced
1 green pepper, diced
2-oz. jar diced pimentos
1 t. dried parsley
1/2 c. sliced black olives
4-oz. can sliced mushrooms,
  drained

3/4 c. milk
2 T. dry white wine or
  chicken broth
10-3/4 oz. can cream of
  mushroom soup
10-3/4 oz. can cream of
  chicken soup
4 c. prepared spaghetti
Garnish: toasted, slivered
  almonds

Reserving 1/4 cup Parmesan cheese, combine all ingredients in a
mixing bowl. Place mixture in a lightly greased 13"x9" baking pan;
sprinkle reserved cheese over top. Bake at 375 degrees for 30 minutes
or until hot and bubbly. Garnish with almonds. Serves 6 to 8.

For a really old-fashioned feel,
let braided rugs
double as tree skirts.

Easy Elegant Turkey

Susan Young
Madison, AL

Moist and so simple to make.

14-lb. turkey
salt and pepper to taste
1 stalk celery, chopped
1 onion, chopped

12 bay leaves
6 sprigs fresh parsley
1/2 c. butter, melted

Pat turkey dry with paper towels; season cavity with salt and pepper. Place celery and onion in cavity. Gently lift skin of turkey breast by inserting fingers under skin. Insert bay leaves and parsley springs. Pull skin back down over turkey. Line a large roasting pan with aluminum foil, leaving enough foil over the sides to cover turkey. Place turkey in roasting pan; pour melted butter over top and salt and pepper to taste. Loosely cover turkey with foil. Bake at 450 degrees for 4-1/2 hours or until a meat thermometer inserted into the thickest part of the inner thigh registers 180 degrees. Remove foil during last hour of baking to brown. Let turkey rest 15 minutes before transferring to a serving platter to slice. Serves 10 to 15.

When guests leave snowy boots at the door, secretly slip in a small gift or two for an unexpected surprise.

Family & Friends Together

Roast Turkey Barbecue Sauce

Verla Monge
Roanoke, IL

I roast a turkey every December and always make this sauce to serve with it. Make it ahead of time if you'd like and just reheat.

1/2 c. water
1/2 c. vinegar
1/2 c. margarine
1-lb. pkg. brown sugar

1 t. Worcestershire sauce
1 t. salt
32-oz. bottle catsup

Combine all ingredients in a saucepan and simmer for 30 minutes. Pour over turkey during the last 30 minutes of baking. Makes about 5 cups.

Tart Cherry Sauce

Donna Dillon
Scottdale, PA

This sauce goes well with turkey and pork.

6-oz. pkg. dried cranberries
3 3-oz. cans tart cherries

2 c. water
1/2 to 1 c. maple sugar

Place the first 3 ingredients in a large stockpot over medium heat; cover and let simmer for 3 hours, stirring occasionally. If mixture becomes too thick, add water to desired consistency. Once berries have popped and cooked, stir in maple sugar to taste. Allow mixture to stand 5 to 10 minutes to thicken. Makes about 3 cups.

Nutty Sweet Potato & Ham Rolls

Carrie Cudney
West Jordan, UT

A new spin on the traditional ham dinner...these won't last long!

15-oz. can sweet potatoes,
    drained and syrup reserved
3 T. brown sugar, packed and
    divided
1/2 c. chopped pecans
1/4 t. ground cloves
8 slices cooked ham
13-1/2 oz. can pineapple tidbits
1 T. vinegar
1 T. cornstarch

Mash the sweet potatoes adding 2 tablespoons reserved syrup, one tablespoon brown sugar, pecans and cloves; mix well. Spread mixture on each ham slice. Roll up each slice jelly-roll style; secure with toothpicks and place in an ungreased 2-quart casserole dish. Combine pineapple with juice, vinegar, remaining brown sugar and cornstarch in a saucepan; cook over low heat, stirring constantly, until thickened. Pour half the sauce over ham rolls. Cover dish and bake at 350 degrees for 15 minutes. Serve with remaining sauce. Serves 4 to 6.

Place a pillar candle in a pie plate, then surround the candle with nostalgic glass ornaments...the retro colors will really sparkle when the candle is lit!

♡ Family & Friends Together ❄

Cheesy Beef & Potatoes

Stacie Bauman
Congerville, IL

Try Pepper Jack cheese for a hotter flavor.

4 c. potatoes, peeled and sliced
1 onion, chopped
1-1/2 t. salt, divided
3/4 t. pepper, divided
1 t. dried parsley
1 lb. ground beef

1/2 c. round buttery crackers,
  crushed
1/4 c. catsup
1/2 c. shredded Cheddar cheese
1/2 c. shredded mozzarella
  cheese

Arrange potatoes and onion in a greased 2-quart casserole dish;
sprinkle with 1/2 teaspoon salt, 1/2 teaspoon pepper and parsley.
Combine ground beef, crushed crackers and remaining salt and pepper
in a mixing bowl; spread over potatoes. Bake at 350 degrees for
45 minutes. Spread catsup over top and sprinkle with cheeses;
continue baking for 15 additional minutes or until cheese is golden.
Serves 6.

Give a Christmas
celebration in a bag! Slip
holiday CD's, ornaments
and homemade candy
inside a festive gift bag
that's sure to be a
welcome hostess gift.

Layered Ravioli Bake

Kim Morris
Collinsville, IL

Make some bread sticks and toss a salad while it's baking.

24-oz. pkg. frozen beef ravioli
15-oz. container ricotta cheese
10-oz. pkg. frozen chopped
    spinach, thawed and drained
1 egg, slightly beaten

1 t. dried basil
32-oz. jar spaghetti sauce,
    divided
3/4 c. grated Parmesan cheese

Cook ravioli according to package directions; drain. Combine ricotta cheese, spinach, egg and basil in a mixing bowl; set aside. Spread one cup spaghetti sauce in the bottom of a 13"x9" baking pan coated with non-stick vegetable spray. Arrange half the ravioli in a single layer over sauce; spread cheese mixture over ravioli. Layer remaining ravioli and remaining sauce on top. Bake at 350 degrees for 30 to 35 minutes or until sauce is bubbly. Sprinkle Parmesan cheese over top and let stand 10 minutes before serving. Serves 6.

GIve little ones a tiny Christmas tree of their very own decorated with a gumdrop garland, stuffed animals and candy canes...it's sure to make their holiday extra special!

Country Chicken Dish

Wendy Lee Pajerrour
Pine Island, NY

There won't be any leftovers!

2 eggs
1 c. milk
10-3/4 oz. can cream of
    chicken soup

...wl. Combine mayonnaise, onion
...mixture over chicken, stirring
...ng mix in the bottom of a
...tick vegetable spray. Arrange
...ning stuffing mix over chicken.
...and milk; pour over stuffing.
...rigerate overnight. Before
...ver top and cover again. Bake at
350 degrees for one hour or until bubbly. Serves 6.

Instead of the usual family photo, send whimsical
greeting cards this year...let everyone make snow
angels side-by-side and then take a picture of the
snow family!

Stuffed Peppers

Cheryl Kiss
Kingsport, TN

Try yellow or red peppers too...they have a slightly sweeter taste.

1 lb. ground beef
1 T. adobe seasoning
2 T. garlic, pressed
1 onion, chopped
6.9-oz. box chicken-flavored
   rice vermicelli mix
8-oz. pkg. mozzarella cheese

1/2 c. grated Parmesan cheese
1 c. bread crumbs
1 egg
6-oz. can tomato paste
6 green peppers
2 cubes chicken bouillon
16-oz. can tomato sauce

Place ground beef, adobe seasoning, garlic and onion in a skillet; cook until beef is browned. Prepare rice mix according to package directions. Combine rice and beef mixture in a mixing bowl; add mozzarella cheese, Parmesan cheese, bread crumbs, egg and tomato paste. Mix well. Slice tops off green peppers; hollow out the insides. Fill a large stockpot with 1-1/2 inches water; add bouillon cubes. Bring to a boil. Place peppers, upside-down, in the pot; cook for 4 minutes. Turn peppers right-side up and cook 4 additional minutes. Remove peppers; place upside-down on paper towels to drain and cool. Once cool, stuff each with beef mixture. Return stuffed peppers to pot with water; add tomato sauce until the liquid reaches the tops of the peppers. Cover and simmer on low heat for one hour. Serves 6.

Somehow not only
for Christmas
But all the long
year through,
The joy that you give
to others
Is the joy that comes
back to you.
-Anonymous

Scrumptious Sides

Sweet Potato Casserole

Karrie Middaugh
Salt Lake City, UT

*A yummy praline streusel is both stirred into the casserole
and sprinkled on top.*

1 c. all-purpose flour
2/3 c. brown sugar, packed
1/4 c. chopped pecans, toasted
1/4 c. margarine
1/2 t. cinnamon
4 sweet potatoes, peeled and
   halved

1/2 c. sugar
1-1/2 t. vanilla extract
1 egg white
5-oz. can fat-free evaporated
   milk

Combine the first 5 ingredients in a small bowl, stirring to form a
streusel; set aside. Place potatoes in a Dutch oven; add water to cover.
Bring to a boil, cover and reduce heat. Simmer 30 minutes or until
potatoes are very tender; drain well. Mash potatoes in a large bowl.
Stir in one cup streusel mixture, sugar, vanilla, egg white and milk.
Spoon into a 2-quart casserole dish coated with non-stick vegetable
spray; top with remaining streusel. Bake at 350 degrees for
45 minutes. Serves 8.

Line up vases filled with white
flowers such as tulips, lilies,
amaryllis or roses. Alongside
the traditional Christmas
green and red, these flowers
make a simple, elegant
table centerpiece.

Scrumptious Sides

Angel Biscuits

Angela Greenhaw
Pensacola, FL

What else can be said? They're heavenly!

2 pkgs. active dry yeast
1/4 c. warm water
5 c. self-rising flour
1/3 c. sugar

1 t. baking soda
1 c. shortening
2 c. buttermilk

Dissolve yeast in warm water; set aside. In a separate bowl, combine flour, sugar and baking soda; cut in shortening to cornmeal consistency. Stir in yeast mixture and buttermilk to form a dough. With oiled hands, roll dough into one-inch balls. Arrange biscuits in a lightly oiled 13"x9" baking pan; bake at 400 degrees for 25 to 30 minutes. Makes about 3 dozen.

Tender Popovers

Gail Prather
Bethel, MN

There's nothing like these delicate popovers spread with real butter.

3 eggs
1-1/4 c. milk

1-1/4 c. all-purpose flour
1/4 t. salt

Beat eggs with an electric mixture on medium speed until light yellow. Add milk; continue beating for one minute. Stir in remaining ingredients; pour batter into greased muffin tins. Bake at 450 degrees for 15 minutes; reduce temperature to 350 degrees, without opening oven door, and continue baking 25 to 30 minutes or until golden. Insert knife into each popover to allow steam to escape. Makes one dozen.

Oodles of Noodles Salad

*Judy Campbell
New Castle, PA*

A crunchy coleslaw that's packed with flavor!

1 c. oil
1/2 c. white vinegar
1/2 c. sugar
2 3-oz. pkgs. beef ramen
   noodles with seasoning
   packets

16-oz. pkg. coleslaw mix
1 c. sunflower seeds
1 bunch green onions, chopped
6-oz. pkg. slivered almonds

Mix together oil, vinegar, sugar and seasoning packets from ramen noodles; refrigerate overnight for flavors to blend. In a large bowl, crush uncooked ramen noodles; stir in coleslaw mix, sunflower seeds, onions and almonds. Pour refrigerated dressing over all, stirring well to combine. Serves 6 to 8.

When time's short, make a warm loaf of Crostini for dinner...it's easy! Slice a loaf of French bread into one-inch diagonal slices. Melt together 1/2 cup olive oil with 1/2 cup butter and coat one side of each slice of bread. Bake in a 300-degree oven for 30 minutes or until toasty.

Cheesy Broccoli Casserole

Dalto

This easy-to-make casserole is great for busy holidays!

2 lbs. broccoli, cut into flowerets
10-3/4 oz. can cream of
    mushroom soup
1/2 c. mayonnaise

1/2 c. shredded Cheddar cheese
1 T. lemon juice
1 c. cheese-flavored crackers,
    crushed

Fill a saucepan with one inch of water; add broccoli and bring to a boil. Reduce heat; cover and simmer until broccoli is crisp-tender, about 5 to 8 minutes. Drain and place in a greased 2-quart casserole dish. In a large bowl, combine soup, mayonnaise, cheese and lemon juice; pour over broccoli. Sprinkle crushed crackers over top. Bake at 350 degrees for 25 to 30 minutes. Serves 6 to 8.

If you live close by a river that's frozen during the holidays, gather up skates, mittens, scarves and hot cider and enjoy a fun-filled afternoon of ice skating!

Mom's Holiday Mac & Cheese

Debbie Roberts
Columbus, IN

*We could always count on Mom to make this dish on Christmas.
We've even been known to eat the leftovers for breakfast!*

8-oz. pkg. elbow macaroni,
  cooked
1/4 c. butter
1/4 c. all-purpose flour
1 t. salt

1/8 t. pepper
2 c. milk
8-oz. pkg. shredded Cheddar
  cheese, divided

Drain macaroni and set aside. Melt butter in a medium saucepan;
remove from heat. Stir in flour, salt and pepper. Gradually stir in
milk; return to heat and bring to a boil. Reduce heat; simmer for one
minute until sauce thickens. Remove from heat. Stir in 1-1/2 cups
cheese and prepared macaroni. Pour mixture into a lightly greased
1-1/2 quart casserole dish. Sprinkle remaining cheese over top. Bake
at 375 degrees for 15 minutes or until cheese is golden. Serves 4 to 6.

Turn a toboggan into a clever wintertime serving table!
Just set it securely on top of a buffet table, toss on a
plaid throw, and then load it up with lots of
salads, sides and breads.

Scrumptious Sides

Buttery Carrots & Onions

Flo Burtnett
Gage, OK

Dad always offered thanks for our food before each meal and his prayer often included "and we thank Thee for all the cares and blessings of life." My 5-year-old nephew loved Dad and often imitated him. When it was his turn to offer thanks, his prayer included "and we thank Thee for all the carrots and blessing of life!"

2 T. butter
3 carrots, grated

1 bunch green onions, chopped
salt to taste

Melt butter in a skillet over medium heat; reduce heat and add carrots and onions. Cover and cook until carrots are crisp-tender, about 3 to 5 minutes. Salt to taste. Serves 4.

Keep a blanket chest by the back door...a great place for keeping winter gear handy! Give it a little personality by painting it red, and then stencilling it with mittens and snowflakes. When it's all dry, just add a coat of spray sealer to the entire bench so the painted designs are protected.

Carry-In Casserole

Judy Cheatham
Brentwood, TN

It seems everyone requests I bring this casserole whenever I'm going to a carry-in. A recipe shared by a dear friend, it's a winner and very easy to prepare.

2 lbs. squash
1 onion, chopped
1 green pepper, chopped
1-oz. pkg. ranch dressing mix
1 c. mayonnaise
1 c. sharp Cheddar cheese

2 eggs, beaten
1 sleeve round buttery crackers, crushed
2 T. butter
Garnish: paprika

Place squash, onion and green pepper in a saucepan; cover with water and bring to a boil. Cover and simmer until vegetables are tender. Drain and mash. Stir in dressing mix, mayonnaise, cheese and eggs; pour mixture into a lightly greased 2-quart casserole dish. In a skillet, brown crushed crackers in butter; sprinkle over casserole. Garnish with paprika. Bake at 300 degrees for 30 minutes. Serves 6 to 8.

Make a centerpiece in seconds…gather lots of old-fashioned glass bulbs and set each one in egg cups, bud bases, fluted glasses or teacups. Grouped together they add sparkle and shine to any table!

Scrumptious Sides

Family Favorite Coleslaw

Susan Estel
New Egypt, NJ

This salad has been a favorite for years. We especially like it on turkey sandwiches, but it's a delicious addition to any family gathering.

1 c. green pepper, diced	4 T. sugar
8 c. coleslaw mix	2 T. mustard
3/4 c. mayonnaise	1/2 t. black pepper
1/2 c. sour cream	1/2 t. celery seed
4 T. vinegar	1 T. dried parsley

Combine green pepper and coleslaw mix in a large bowl. Whisk together the remaining ingredients in a separate bowl; pour over coleslaw mixture. Cover and chill 3 to 4 hours. Serves 8 to 10.

March a set of colorful wooden nutcrackers up the stairs…a sweet, nostalgic greeting!

Fruity Walnut Salad

Maureen Jarvis
Covian, CA

A "must-have" at any holiday gathering.

3-oz. pkg. lemon gelatin mix
3-oz. pkg. lime gelatin mix
1/2 t. salt
1 c. boiling water
1 c. mayonnaise
12-oz. can evaporated milk

2 c. cottage cheese
20-oz. can crushed pineapple,
   drained
1 c. celery, diced
1 c. chopped walnuts

Dissolve gelatin and salt in boiling water in a ungreased 13"x9" baking pan; mix in mayonnaise. Stir in remaining ingredients and chill until set. Serves 10 to 12.

Refreshing Raspberry Salad

Michelle Riley
Gering, NE

Delicious spread with a thin layer of sour cream,
then topped with mini marshmallows.

6-oz. pkg. raspberry gelatin mix
1 c. hot water
1 c. cold water

16-oz. can applesauce
2 10-oz. pkgs. frozen
   raspberries

Dissolve gelatin mix in hot water in a 9"x9" baking pan; stir in cold water. Add applesauce and raspberries. Cover and refrigerate until set. Serves 6 to 8.

Use a sewing needle threaded with fishing line
to make the prettiest gumdrop garland!

Nutty Banana Bread

Stacie Barth
Salt Lake City, UT

*Adding cream cheese to the batter makes this banana bread
extra moist and extra delicious!*

1/2 c. butter, softened
8-oz. pkg. cream cheese,
  softened
1-1/4 c. sugar
2 eggs
1 c. bananas, mashed
1 t. vanilla extract

2-1/4 c. all-purpose flour
1-1/2 t. baking powder
1/2 t. baking soda
3/4 c. chopped pecans
2 T. brown sugar, packed
2 t. cinnamon

Cream together butter and cream cheese in a mixing bowl; gradually
add sugar, beating until light and fluffy. Add eggs, one at a time,
beating well after each addition. Stir in mashed bananas and vanilla.
Add flour, baking powder and baking soda; mix until just moist. In a
small bowl, combine pecans, brown sugar and cinnamon. Divide half
the banana batter between 2 greased and floured 8"x4" loaf pans;
sprinkle pecan mixture over batter. Pour remaining batter over top.
Bake at 350 degrees for 35 minutes or until a toothpick inserted into
centers comes out clean. Makes 2 loaves.

A wide satin ribbon draped over the back of each chair
makes a quick-as-a-wink placecard. Just rubber stamp
the guest's name on each ribbon!

d Corn Pudding

Jodi King
Friendship, MD

*ldn't be Christmas without this dish on our
table...I usually double the recipe!*

2 eggs, beaten
1/4 to 1/2 c. sugar
2 slices bread, crusts trimmed

14-3/4 oz. can creamed corn
1/2 c. evaporated milk
1 t. vanilla extract

Mix together eggs and sugar; cube bread and add to mixture. Stir
in corn, milk and vanilla. Pour mixture into a buttered 1-1/2 quart
casserole dish. Bake at 350 degrees for one hour. Serves 4 to 6.

*Get the whole family jaunty, matching long-johns for
silly, but memorable Christmas pictures!*

Scrumptious Sides

Sweet-Tart Green Bean Salad

*Darlene Martin
Cleveland, TN*

This salad marinates overnight so the delicious flavors blend.

14-1/2 oz. can French-style
   green beans, drained
14-1/2 oz. can baby peas,
   drained
1 green pepper, chopped
2 onions, sliced

2-oz. jar pimentos
1/2 c. oil
1 c. white vinegar
1 T. salt
1 c. sugar
1 T. water

Combine first 5 ingredients in a large bowl; set aside. In a separate bowl, mix together remaining ingredients; pour over green bean mixture. Cover and refrigerate 12 to 24 hours. Drain for one hour before serving. Serves 6 to 8.

Snowflakes cut from paper lace,
A fragile angel hung in place
Within the evergreen's embrace,
Temptations for a cat to chase.
-D.A.W.

Snowflake Bread

Vickie

*Golden honey-glazed loaves with a snowflake design...so
pretty for Christmas dinner.*

3/4 c. milk
1/2 c. butter
1/2 t. salt
1 pkg. active dry yeast
1/4 c. warm water
4-1/2 to 5 c. all-purpose flour,
    divided

1/4 c. honey
2 eggs
1-1/2 t. anise seed, crushed
2 t. vanilla extract

Stir together milk, butter and salt in a saucepan; cook over medium
heat until smooth, about 5 to 7 minutes. Cool slightly. In a mixing
bowl, dissolve yeast in warm water; add milk mixture, 2 cups flour,
honey, eggs, anise seed and vanilla. Beat with an electric mixer until
smooth. Stir in remaining flour to form a soft dough. Turn dough onto
a lightly floured surface; knead until smooth. Place in a greased bowl,
turning dough to coat; cover and let rise until double in bulk. Punch
dough down and divide in half. Form each half into 7-1/2 inch round
loaves; place on greased baking sheets. Cover dough and let rise until
almost double in bulk. Use a knife to make a snowflake design in each
loaf. Bake loaves at 350 degrees for 20 minutes. Brush glaze over
loaves; return to oven for 5 to 10 minutes or until tops are golden.
Serves 10 to 12.

Glaze:

1 egg, beaten
1 T. honey

1 T. water

Stir all ingredients together.

Just for fun, hang mittens on the mantel instead of stockings!

Scrumptious Sides

Great-Grandma's Stuffing

Lori Van Aken
Arvada, CO

My Italian great-grandmother would make this dish for holidays and special occasions. It's almost a meal in itself!

2 T. olive oil
3 cloves garlic, minced
1 lb. mushrooms, sliced
5 stalks celery, chopped
1 onion, chopped
4-oz. can sliced black olives

8-oz. stick pepperoni, chopped
3/4 c. fresh parsley, chopped
1 t. poultry seasoning
peppery to taste
15 to 18 slices bread, torn
1-1/2 cubes chicken bouillon

Heat oil in a large skillet; add garlic, mushrooms, celery and onion. Sauté for 5 minutes over medium heat. Add olives, pepperoni, parsley, poultry seasoning and pepper; sauté 5 additional minutes. Place bread in a lightly greased 13"x9" baking pan; mix in sautéed mixture until moistened. Gradually stir in chicken bouillon. Bake at 325 degrees for 40 to 45 minutes. Serves 4 to 6.

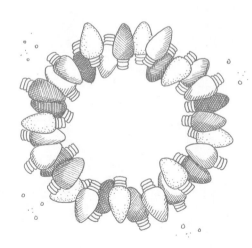

For the prettiest wreath, use craft glue to secure old-fashioned Christmas bulbs to a foam wreath form...so colorful and clever!

Holiday Yams

Leah-Anne Schnapp
Effort, PA

One of my favorite recipes for holiday cooking...I can't get away without making it!

29-oz. can sliced peaches
2 T. cornstarch
2/3 c. brown sugar, packed
16-oz. can cranberry sauce

1 t. cinnamon
4 T. butter
2 40-oz. cans yams, drained

Drain peaches, reserving juice. Mix together cornstarch with 1/4 cup reserved juice. Pour remaining juice in a saucepan; mix in brown sugar, cranberry sauce, cinnamon and butter. Cook over medium heat until butter is melted, stirring constantly. Add cornstarch mixture; heat until thickened. Add yams and heat for 10 minutes. Stir in peaches, heating 5 additional minutes. Serves 10 to 12.

Tiny mittens, hats and baby socks are so sweet on a tiny white tree...set it in the nursery for little ones to enjoy!

Scrumptious

Almond-Poppy Seed Bread

Just the right size for gift-giving!

3 c. all-purpose flour
1-1/2 t. salt
1-1/2 t. baking powder
2-1/2 c. sugar
1-1/2 c. milk

2-1/2 t. poppy see~
3 eggs
1-1/2 t. vanilla extract
1-1/2 t. almond extract
1-1/4 c. oil

Mix together all ingredients. Grease six, 4-1/2"x2-1/2" mini loaf pans; fill each 3/4 full. Bake at 350 degrees for one hour or until golden. Makes 6 loaves.

A hollowed-out round loaf of bread is terrific for holding dinner rolls or salads. If no one nibbles on it after it's empty, share it as a Christmas treat for the birds!

Buttermilk Cornbread

Kelly delCid
Troy, OH

Try pouring batter in muffin tins or old-fashioned corn stick molds.

2 c. cornmeal
1/2 c. all-purpose flour
1 t. baking powder
1/2 t. baking soda

1 t. salt
1 egg, lightly beaten
2 c. buttermilk
2 T. oil

Mix together first 5 ingredients; set aside. Combine egg, buttermilk and oil; add to dry ingredients. Pour batter into a hot, well-greased 9-inch skillet. Bake at 450 degrees for 15 to 20 minutes or until golden. Serves 8 to 12.

Tangy Black Bean Salad

Elizabeth Talmage
San Clemente, CA

A nice change of pace from traditional salads.

2 15-1/2 oz. cans black beans,
   drained
1 green pepper, chopped
1 red onion, chopped
1/2 c. cilantro, chopped
1/2 c. olive oil

1/2 t. lime zest
1/2 t. red pepper
1/2 c. lime juice
1/2 t. cumin
salt and pepper to taste

Combine first 4 ingredients in a large bowl. Combine remaining ingredients in a separate bowl; pour over bean mixture. Chill 3 to 4 hours. Serves 6 to 8.

Be a kid again…make snow angels!

Scrumptious Sides

Barley Quick Bread

Sherry Saarinen
Hancock, MI

In November of 2000, my sisters and I traveled to Finland to see the town where our ancestors had once lived. Prior to leaving, we collected letters from some of the children in our hometown to take to Santa Claus. It was there in Santa's kitchen at Santa Park that we enjoyed this delicious bread. We will always cherish the memory of Santa's kindness and the sweet aroma of freshly baked Finnish bread.

2 c. all-purpose flour	1 t. baking powder
1/2 c. pearled barley, uncooked	1/2 t. baking soda
1 t. salt	1 c. buttermilk
1 t. sugar	1/4 c. butter, melted

Mix together first 6 ingredients; stir in buttermilk. Turn dough onto a lightly floured surface; knead. Roll dough into an oval shape, 1/2 to 3/4-inch thick. Score dough with a knife and prick with a fork; place on a lightly greased and floured baking sheet. Bake at 375 degrees for 15 to 25 minutes. Cool on a wire rack and brush with melted butter. Serves 4 to 6.

Vintage candleholders...just stack 3 cast iron architectural stars and set a dripless taper inside!

Cheesy Cabbage Bake

Phyllis Fulks
Beattyville, KY

*An easy side dish that can bake while you and the kids
build a snowman!*

1 head cabbage, shredded
2 T. butter
2 T. all-purpose flour
1-1/4 c. milk, warmed

salt and pepper to taste
10 slices American cheese
1 sleeve round buttery crackers,
   crushed

Place cabbage in a large saucepan; cover with water. Boil 10 minutes
or until tender; drain. Melt butter in a small saucepan; stir in flour
and cook until paste forms and bubbles, about 2 minutes. Add milk,
stirring as sauce thickens; bring to a boil. Add salt and pepper;
reduce heat and cook for 2 to 3 minutes, stirring constantly. Coat a
13"x9" baking pan with non-stick vegetable spray; add a layer of
sauce, cheese and cabbage. Repeat layer. Cover pan with aluminum
foil and bake at 350 degrees for 25 minutes. Top with crushed
crackers; bake uncovered for 5 additional minutes. Serves 8 to 10.

*The street cars are like frosted cakes
All covered up, with cold snowflakes.
And everywhere the people go,
With faces tickled by the snow.*
-Dorothy Aldis

Scrumptious Sides

Seafood Pasta Salad

Weda Mosellie
Phillipsburg, NJ

*This is a great salad for holiday gatherings because
it can be made a day ahead.*

1-lb. pkg. bowtie pasta, cooked
1 c. broccoli, chopped and
   blanched
3 T. olive oil
1 T. lemon juice
salt and pepper to taste
1 T. grated Parmesan cheese

1 t. garlic powder
1 t. fresh dill
1 t. dried oregano
10-oz. pkg. imitation crabmeat
1 carrot, julienned
10-oz. can black olives, drained
1 onion, chopped

Drain and rinse pasta and broccoli; set aside to cool. Stir together next
7 ingredients in a large mixing bowl. Add crabmeat, pasta and
broccoli; toss gently until well coated. Add remaining ingredients and
toss; cover and chill for one hour or overnight. Serves 8 to 10.

*Throughout the year, keep an eye out at tag sales for
old paper maché candy-container boots and
ticking-stripe fabric candy canes...old-fashioned
decorations that are still sweet today.*

Macaroni Casserole

Brooke & Tina Knotts
Gooseberry Patch

This hearty casserole is one of our family's favorite recipes because it brings to mind all the comforts of home.

3-oz. pkg. dried chopped beef
2 c. prepared elbow macaroni
4 eggs, hard-boiled, peeled
    and chopped
2 10-3/4 oz. cans cream of
    mushroom soup

2-1/2 to 3 c. milk
8-oz. pkg. pasteurized process
    cheese spread, cubed

Combine all ingredients in a large mixing bowl; mix well. Spoon mixture into a greased 13"x9" baking pan. Bake at 350 degrees for 45 minutes. Serves 6 to 8.

Think of a few questions to share during Christmas dinner. What's a favorite holiday memory? Does anyone have a Christmas wish this year? What about a New Year's wish? It's a nice way to share sweet memories and catch up with friends & family during this special time of year.

Scrumptious Sides

Festive Corn Bake

Nancy Schroeder
McPherson, KS

A crispy, buttery topping sets this corn casserole apart from the rest!

15-1/4 oz. can corn, drained
14-1/2 oz. can French-style
   green beans, drained
8-oz. container sour cream
1 onion, chopped
10-3/4 oz. can cream of
   celery soup

1 sleeve round buttery crackers,
   crushed
1/2 c. butter, melted
1 c. sliced almonds

Mix together corn and green beans; spread in an ungreased 2-quart casserole dish. Stir together sour cream, onion and soup; spread over vegetables. Mix crackers, butter and almonds together; spread over soup layer. Bake at 350 degrees for 30 minutes or until bubbly. Serves 6.

Rubber stamp wide ribbon with holiday greetings such as "Joy," "Ho, Ho, Ho" and "Don't open until Christmas!" Tied around packages, it's a quick & easy way to make giftwrap more fun!

Pineapple-Macadamia Nut Bread

Laurie Parrott
La Habra, CA

Nut bread with a tropical twist!

3 c. whole macadamia nuts
15-1/4 oz. can pineapple
   chunks, drained
3-1/2 oz. can flaked coconut
3/4 c. all-purpose flour

3/4 c. sugar
1/2 t. baking powder
1/2 t. salt
3 eggs
1 t. vanilla extract

Combine nuts, pineapple and coconut in a large bowl; mix well. Sift together flour, sugar, baking powder and salt; add to nut mixture. Mix all until nuts and fruit are completely coated with flour. Beat eggs until foamy and add vanilla; stir into nut mixture. Spoon batter into a greased 8"x4" loaf pan lined with wax paper. Bake at 325 degrees for 50 to 60 minutes or until center tests done. Remove from pan and cool completely. Wrap in foil or plastic wrap and refrigerate until serving. Serves 6 to 8.

If the fireplace isn't used during the holidays, it can still look warm and inviting. Fill an empty grate with snowy white birch logs or candles of every shape and size. Lighting them gives a cozy glow to any room.

Scrumptious Sides

Spiced Fruit

Elaine Nichols
Mesa, AZ

This is always a Christmas favorite with our family because it's a nice change from the usual vegetable side dishes.

29-oz. can sliced peaches
15-1/4 oz. can apricot halves
3/4 c. brown sugar, packed
1/2 c. white vinegar
4 cinnamon sticks

1 t. whole cloves
1 T. whole allspice
20-oz. can pineapple chunks,
   drained

Drain the juice from the peaches and apricots into a large saucepan; add brown sugar, vinegar, cinnamon sticks, cloves and allspice. Bring to a boil and boil for 5 minutes. Add pineapple chunks, peaches and apricots to the saucepan; simmer until fruit is warm. Remove cinnamon sticks and cloves. Serves 6 to 8.

Christmas is for having fun, so gather the whole family in a photo with Santa…a greeting card that will have everyone smiling!

Flaky Biscuits

Susan Young
Madison, AL

*Topped with butter or drizzled with honey, these
are at home on any dinner table!*

2 c. all-purpose flour   1/3 c. shortening
3 T. baking powder   3/4 c. milk
1 t. salt

Sift flour, baking powder and salt into a large bowl; cut in shortening
to resemble coarse crumbs. Gently stir in milk until just blended. Turn
dough out onto a floured surface; knead one to 2 minutes. Roll dough
to 1/2-inch thickness; cut into biscuits. Place biscuits on ungreased
baking sheets; bake at 425 degrees for 12 to 15 minutes. Makes
one dozen.

All during December keep favorite Christmas books in
a basket that's close at hand when it's bedtime for little
ones. Snuggle together under a fuzzy blanket and read
a story together…what a special way to
end the day.

Scrumptious Sides

Miss Polly's Perfect Potatoes

Gaybrielle Ray
Springfield, OH

I named this recipe after my daughter. She was my critic for a year of taste-testing to perfect this recipe. She loves it!

5 lbs. red skin potatoes
1/2 c. butter
12-oz. container French-onion chip dip
8-oz. pkg. cream cheese
1 t. salt
1 T. pepper
12-oz. pkg. shredded sharp Cheddar cheese
6-oz. can French-fried onions

Place potatoes in a large stockpot; add water to cover. Bring to a boil, cooking until potatoes are tender; drain. Mash potatoes with butter, dip, cream cheese, salt and pepper. Spoon potatoes into a buttered 13"x9" baking pan; top with shredded cheese. Bake at 400 degrees for 10 to 15 minutes or until cheese is bubbly. Sprinkle onions over top and bake for one to 2 additional minutes. Serves 6 to 8.

Giving a little seamstress a gift of child-size sewing supplies? Make them extra special by writing her name and drawing cheery flowers, butterflies and ladybugs on the scissor handles using a paint marker.

Eggplant Parmesan

Tony Bonina
Westerville, OH

Deliciously cheesy and surprisingly easy!

1 eggplant, peeled
1 c. whole-wheat bread crumbs
1 t. dried oregano
1 T. fresh parsley, chopped
salt and pepper to taste
1/2 c. water

2 c. marinara sauce, divided
2 c. shredded mozzarella cheese,
  divided
1 tomato, sliced and divided
1 c. grated Parmesan cheese,
  divided

Cut eggplant crosswise into 1/4-inch thick slices. Mix together bread crumbs, oregano, parsley, salt and pepper in a shallow dish. Dip eggplant slices in water to dampen, then dip in bread crumbs to coat. Heat coated slices in a skillet coated with non-stick vegetable spray; cook over medium-high heat for one minute on each side. Arrange browned eggplant slices in a single layer on a baking sheet coated with non-stick vegetable spray; bake at 350 degrees for 30 minutes, turning once after 15 minutes. Spoon 1/2 cup marinara sauce into an 8"x8" baking pan coated with non-stick vegetable spray; arrange a single layer of browned eggplant slices on top. Layer 1/2 cup sauce, 1/2 cup mozzarella cheese, half the tomato slices and 1/2 cup Parmesan over eggplant; cover with 1/2 cup sauce. Repeat layers starting with eggplant, followed by sauce, mozzarella, tomatoes, Parmesan and sauce; top with remaining mozzarella. Cover with aluminum foil and bake at 350 degrees for 30 minutes. Allow to stand for 5 minutes before serving. Serves 4 to 6.

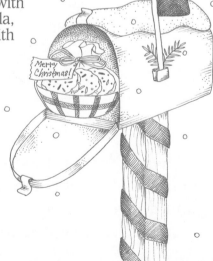

Don't forget a sweet treat for the letter carrier...what a welcome surprise when the mailbox is opened!

Scrumptious Sides

Mushroom-Stuffed Tomatoes

Jo Ann

Baked tomatoes are a tasty, old-fashioned dish, and this updated version stuffed with mushrooms is wonderful!

6 tomatoes
1-1/2 c. mushrooms, chopped
3 T. butter, divided
2 egg yolks
1/2 c. sour cream

1/4 c. plus 3 T. bread crumbs, divided
1 t. salt
1/4 t. dried thyme
1/8 t. pepper

Cut a thin slice off the top of each tomato; leaving a 1/2-inch shell, scoop out pulp and reserve one cup. Place tomatoes upside down on paper towels to drain. Chop reserved pulp and set aside. Sauté mushrooms in 2 tablespoons butter in a skillet. Combine egg yolks and sour cream; add to mushrooms. Mix in 1/4 cup bread crumbs, salt, thyme, pepper and reserved tomato pulp. Simmer mixture until thickened, about one minute. Spoon 1/3 cupful mixture into each tomato. Arrange tomatoes in an ungreased 11"x7" baking pan. Melt remaining butter and toss with remaining bread crumbs; sprinkle over stuffed tomatoes. Bake at 350 degrees for 30 to 35 minutes. Serves 6.

Kids will be the apple of a teacher's eye with this gift! Place a shiny red apple in the center of an old-fashioned apple baker. Use a long length of ribbon to hold the apple in the dish and tie the ribbon ends in a big bow...don't forget to add the recipe!

5-Bean Bake

Connie Croak
Lock Haven, PA

Filled with so many good things, this side dish is always a hit!

1 lb. bacon, sliced into one-inch
 pieces
1 lb. ground beef
1 onion, chopped
15-1/2 oz. can kidney beans
15-1/2 oz. can butter beans,
 drained
14-1/2 oz. can green beans,
 drained

15-1/2 oz. can Great Northern
 beans
16-oz. can pork & beans
1/4 c. sugar
3/4 c. brown sugar, packed
1 c. catsup
2 t. vinegar
2 t. mustard

Combine bacon, beef and onion in a large skillet; cook until browned.
Drain. Combine beef mixture with remaining ingredients, mixing well.
Pour mixture into an ungreased 13"x9" baking pan. Bake at
350 degrees for one hour. Serves 10 to 12.

Thread alphabet beads on embroidery floss
and knot the ends together on the back of a package.
Spell out names or holiday greetings for a
personalized package in minutes!

Scrumptious Sides

San Francisco Salad

Marilyn Rogers
Port Townsend, WA

Loaded with flavor, this versatile salad can be served warm or cold.

6.9-oz. pkg. chicken-flavored
  rice vermicelli mix
6-oz. jar marinated artichoke
  hearts

4-oz. can sliced black olives
2 green onions, chopped
1/2 c. mayonnaise
1/2 t. curry powder

Prepare rice mix according to package directions. Drain artichokes, reserving liquid, and chop. Add artichokes, olives and onions to prepared rice. In a separate bowl, blend together mayonnaise, artichoke liquid and curry powder; stir into rice mixture. Serve warm or chilled. Serves 4 to 6.

The snow is soft,
and how it squashes!
"Galumph, galumph!"
go my galoshes.
-Eunice Tietjens

Delicious Greek Stuffing

Denise Picard
Venture, CA

It's always fun to try a new recipe to serve alongside traditional ones.
Add this to your holiday buffet...it just might become a favorite!

1 lb. ground beef
1 onion, chopped
1 c. instant rice, uncooked

2 c. chicken broth
1/2 c. raisins
8-oz. can tomato sauce

Brown ground beef and onion in a large skillet; drain. Combine beef mixture, rice, chicken broth, raisins and tomato sauce in a stockpot; cover and cook until liquid is absorbed, about 20 minutes. Makes 8 servings.

A rustic twig chair that sits empty all winter can be
turned into a welcome greeting for family & friends.
Gather armloads of greens, berries and pine cones,
arrange them in a sap bucket or a painted bushel
basket and place in a chair by the door.

Ho-Ho-Holiday Goodies

Baked Candied Apples

Pam Caldwell
Hickory, PA

Apples in sweet cinnamon sauce...oh-so yummy!

16 to 20 apples, peeled, cored
   and halved
1 c. sugar
2 T. cornstarch

2 c. boiling water
2 T. butter
1 t. vanilla extract
1 c. red cinnamon candies

Place the apple halves in an ungreased 13"x9" baking pan; cover with plastic wrap. Mix sugar and cornstarch in a saucepan; pour boiling water over top, whisking to blend. Heat mixture until boiling. Add butter, vanilla and cinnamon candies. Cook and stir over low heat until candies are melted. Uncover apples and pour sauce over top. Bake at 350 degrees for 20 to 30 minutes. Serves 10 to 12.

Make holiday celebration sticks to tuck inside goodie bags...so good for nibbling on! Pour 2-inch wide rows of red, green and white sprinkles side-by-side on wax paper. Dip pretzel rods in melted white chocolate, and then quickly roll in sprinkles to get a striped effect. Chill pretzels on wax paper until chocolate is firm.

Ho-Ho-Holiday Goodies

Holiday Thumbprint Cookies

Lori Triplett
Westminster, MD

Use green or red food coloring to tint the icing, or stir in 1/4 teaspoon peppermint extract in place of vanilla for the taste of candy canes.

1 c. butter, softened
3/4 c. cornstarch
1/3 c. powdered sugar

1 c. all-purpose flour
Garnish: sliced almonds

Beat butter with an electric mixer on low speed until creamy. Gradually add cornstarch and powdered sugar; increase speed to medium and beat until fluffy. Stir in flour. Cover and chill dough for 45 minutes to one hour. Roll dough into one-inch balls and place 1-1/2 inches apart on ungreased baking sheets. Indent the top of each cookie with a thumbprint. Bake at 350 degrees for 10 to 12 minutes. Cool, then top each with icing. Garnish with sliced almonds. Makes 2 dozen.

Cream Cheese Icing:

3-oz. pkg. cream cheese,
    softened
1 c. powdered sugar

1 t. vanilla extract
Optional: 3 to 4 drops food
    coloring

Blend cream cheese with powdered sugar until creamy and smooth. Mix in vanilla and food coloring if desired.

And he puzzled three hours, 'till his puzzler was sore.
Then the Grinch thought of something
he hadn't before! "Maybe Christmas," he thought,
"doesn't come from a store. Maybe Christmas,
perhaps means a little bit more!"
-Dr. Seuss

Chocolatey Toffee Cake

Jana Marstall
Emporia, KS

Chocolate, caramel and toffee...a winning combination!

18-1/2 oz. pkg. German
    chocolate cake mix
14-oz. can sweetened
    condensed milk
12-oz. jar caramel ice cream
    topping

8-oz. container frozen whipped
    topping, thawed
3 chocolate-covered toffee candy
    bars, crushed
1/2 c. chopped pecans

Prepare and bake cake according to package directions in a
13"x9" baking pan. Poke holes in the top of the cake with a large fork
as soon as it is removed from the oven. Immediately pour sweetened
condensed milk over top and let stand until milk has soaked into the
holes. Repeat process with caramel ice cream topping. Let cake cool
completely. Before serving, frost with whipped topping and sprinkle
crushed candy bars and pecans over top. Serves 10 to 12.

For a beautiful cake garnish, freeze whole cranberries,
then roll in coarse white sugar and arrange, frozen, on a
cake. As the cranberries thaw, they'll have a
beautiful frosty look.

Ho-Ho-Holiday Goodies

Sugar-Dusted Pecan Squares

Tamara Lucas
Guysville, OH

Be sure to include these at your Christmas cookie exchange!

2 T. butter
1 c. brown sugar, packed
5 T. all-purpose flour
1/8 t. baking soda

1 c. chopped pecans
2 eggs
1 t. vanilla extract
Garnish: powdered sugar

Melt butter in an 8"x8" baking pan, tilting to coat. Mix together brown sugar, flour, baking soda and pecans in a small bowl; set aside. In a separate bowl, beat eggs; stir in brown sugar mixture and vanilla. Pour mixture over melted butter in pan; do not stir. Bake at 350 degrees for 20 minutes. Remove, cool slightly and cut into squares. Sprinkle lightly with powdered sugar. Makes 1-1/2 dozen.

Nestle a few cookies in a dainty teacup. Place the cup on a matching saucer and wrap up in tissue paper. Top with a bow and note that reads, "I thought this might be your cup of tea." Any friend will love it!

Santa's Favorite Sugar Cookies

Nicole Lyons
Huntington Beach, CA

*Spend an afternoon making cookies with the kids...they'll
love adding the colorful sprinkles!*

1 c. powdered sugar	1 t. salt
1 c. sugar	1 t. baking soda
2 eggs	4-1/2 c. all-purpose flour
1 c. oil	2 t. vanilla extract
1 c. butter-flavored shortening	Colorful sugar, sprinkles
1 t. cream of tartar	and jimmies

Cream sugars, eggs, oil and shortening in a large bowl. Sift together
dry ingredients in a separate bowl, then add to creamed mixture. Stir
in vanilla. Cover and refrigerate dough for 2 to 3 hours. Roll chilled
dough into 1-1/2 inch balls; place on lightly greased baking sheets.
Flatten each with a glass bottom that has been dipped in sugar.
Sprinkle colorful sugar, sprinkles and jimmies over cookies. Bake at
350 degrees for 10 to 15 minutes or until edges are lightly golden.
Cool cookies on a wire rack. Makes 2 to 3 dozen.

*Dip half (or all!) of Santa's Favorite Sugar Cookies in
melted chocolate for an irresistible chocolatey
sugar cookie!*

Chocolate-Cherry Brownies

Stephanie Raap
Cedar Rapids, IA

If you love chocolate-covered cherries, try these brownies!

1/2 c. butter
3 1-oz. sqs. unsweetened
    baking chocolate
2/3 c. all-purpose flour
1/2 t. baking powder
1/4 t. salt

2 eggs
1 c. sugar
1-1/2 t. vanilla extract
3/4 c. maraschino cherries,
    drained and juice reserved

Melt butter and chocolate together in a saucepan over low heat; set aside. In a separate bowl, combine flour, baking powder and salt. Beat eggs in a separate bowl; add sugar and vanilla. Stir chocolate mixture into egg mixture. Slice the cherries in half, then add to chocolate mixture. Stir in dry ingredients. Pour batter into a greased 8"x8" baking pan. Bake at 350 degrees for 35 to 40 minutes. Cool; spread icing over top. Cut into squares. Makes 8 to 10 servings.

Icing:

2 T. butter, softened
1 c. powdered sugar
3 T. baking cocoa

reserved maraschino
    cherry juice

Blend butter, powdered sugar and cocoa together; add cherry juice to reach desired spreading consistency.

Remember to use jelly-roll pans only for bar cookies…other types of cookies won't bake evenly in a pan with sides.

Spicy Pumpkin-Raisin Cookies

Andrea Cline
Wooster, OH

Pour yourself a big glass of icy milk and enjoy!

1 c. shortening
1 c. sugar
1 c. canned pumpkin
1 egg
2 c. all-purpose flour

1 t. baking soda
1/2 t. salt
1 t. cinnamon
1 c. raisins

Cream shortening, sugar and pumpkin in a mixing bowl; blend in egg. Sift together flour, baking soda, salt and cinnamon; blend into pumpkin mixture. Fold in raisins. Drop by teaspoonfuls onto ungreased baking sheets. Bake at 375 degrees for 10 to 12 minutes. Spread frosting on warm cookies. Makes about 3 dozen.

Frosting:

3 T. butter
4 t. milk
1/2 c. brown sugar, packed

1 c. powdered sugar
3/4 t. vanilla extract

Combine butter, milk and brown sugar in a saucepan over low heat, stirring until dissolved. Cool. Mix in powdered sugar and vanilla.

Leftover canned pumpkin? Try stirring it into softened vanilla ice cream for a frosty treat.

Homemade Eggnog

Rebecca Ferguson
Carlisle, AR

There's nothing like the taste of homemade eggnog...sprinkle with cinnamon or nutmeg before serving.

2/3 c. sugar
4 egg yolks
1/2 t. salt
4 c. milk
8 c. half-and-half
nutmeg to taste

1 pt. whipping cream, chilled
3 T. sugar
2 t. vanilla extract
Garnish: frozen whipped
   topping, thawed

Beat sugar into egg yolks in a saucepan; add salt and stir in milk. Cook mixture over medium heat, stirring constantly, until mixture coats the back of a metal spoon. Remove from heat and set pan in ice water to cool quickly. Pour through a sieve to remove any lumps. Add half-and-half to cooled mixture; sprinkle with nutmeg. In a separate bowl whip cream with sugar and vanilla; fold into egg mixture. Stir well before serving. Serve with a dollop of whipping cream. Makes 12 servings.

For a delicious eggnog punch, combine one quart eggnog, 2 pints softened peppermint ice cream and one cup ginger ale...it's so delicious!

Best-Ever Christmas Cut-Outs

Shirley McGlin
Black Creek, WI

I have been making these for 30 years and they are the best I've found. You can sprinkle them with sugar before baking or frost and decorate after cooling.

1 c. butter, softened
1-1/2 c. powdered sugar
1 egg
1 t. vanilla extract
1/2 t. almond extract

2-1/2 c. all-purpose flour
1 t. baking soda
1 t. cream of tartar
Optional: sugar

Mix together butter, powdered sugar, egg, vanilla and almond extract. Blend in flour, baking soda and cream of tartar. Cover dough and chill for 2 to 3 hours. Divide dough in half; roll one half on a floured surface to 1/8-inch thickness. Cut with cookie cutters; sprinkle with sugar if desired and place on lightly greased baking sheets. Repeat with remaining half of dough. Bake at 375 degrees for 7 to 8 minutes or until lightly golden. Makes about 5 dozen.

Pretty plates in a twinkling…use a paper punch to make holes, in sets of two about one inch apart, along the edge of a pretty paper plate. Weave ribbon through the holes and tie the ends in a bow. Pile on the cookies for a deliciously welcome treat!

Ho-Ho-Holiday Goodies

Peppermint Pinwheels

Kathy McLaren
Visalia, CA

The prettiest cookies for the holidays!

1/2 c. shortening
1/2 c. butter, softened
1-1/4 c. sugar, divided
1 egg
1-1/2 t. almond extract
1 t. vanilla extract
2-1/2 c. all-purpose flour

1 t. salt
1/2 t. red food coloring
2 t. egg white powder
1/4 c. water
1/4 c. peppermint candy sticks, crushed

Mix together shortening, butter, one cup sugar, egg, almond and vanilla extract. Sift together flour and salt; blend into butter mixture. Divide dough in half and blend red food coloring into one half. Chill both halves until firm. Roll light dough on a lightly floured surface to form a 12"x12" square. Roll red half to the same size and lay on top of light dough. Roll the double layer with a rolling pin to 1/16-inch thickness. Tightly roll up jelly-roll style; chill for one hour. Slice chilled dough into 1/8-inch thick cookies. Place on ungreased baking sheets; bake at 375 degrees for 9 minutes or until lightly golden. Mix together egg white powder and water; brush on warm cookies. Mix together crushed candy and remaining sugar; sprinkle on top of each cookie. Makes 2 to 3 dozen.

Giftwrap in a snap!.
Fold down the top of a
goodie-filled treat bag,
punch two holes, one inch
apart, in the center of the
fold and slip a candy cane
through the holes...simple!

Apple-Pecan Cobbler

Dianne Gregory
Sheridan, AR

Top servings with a big dollop of whipped cream or a scoop of vanilla ice cream...what a way to end a meal!

4 c. apples, thinly sliced
1-1/2 c. sugar, divided
1/2 t. cinnamon
3/4 c. chopped pecans, divided
1 c. all-purpose flour

1 t. baking powder
1 t. salt
1 egg, beaten
1/2 c. evaporated milk
1/3 c. butter, melted

Arrange apple slices in an even layer in the bottom of a greased 2-quart casserole dish. Mix together 1/2 cup sugar, cinnamon and 1/2 cup pecans in a small bowl; sprinkle mixture over apples. In a separate bowl, sift together flour, remaining sugar, baking powder and salt; set aside. In a separate bowl, whisk together egg, milk and butter; add to flour mixture all at once. Stir until smooth. Pour mixture over apples and sprinkle top with remaining pecans. Bake at 325 degrees for 55 minutes. Serves 8.

Spoon all the dry ingredients for Apple-Pecan Cobbler into separate plastic zipping bags and nestle along with 4 shiny apples in a retro-style plaid lunch box. Tie a recipe card to the handle for a gift anyone is sure to love!

Ho-Ho-Holiday Goodies

Walnut-Topped Pumpkin Squares

Carrie Cudney
West Jordan, UT

A crumb crust and nutty topping make this anything but ordinary.

1-3/4 c. all-purpose flour
1/3 c. sugar
1/3 c. brown sugar, packed
1 c. butter
1/2 c. chopped walnuts
2 c. canned pumpkin
14-oz. can sweetened
    condensed milk

2 eggs
1 t. allspice
1/2 t. salt
Garnish: frozen whipped
    topping, thawed

Combine flour and sugars in a mixing bowl; cut in butter until crumbly. Reserve one cup crumb mixture; add nuts and set aside. Press remaining crumb mixture firmly on the bottom and halfway up the sides of a lightly greased 12"x7" baking pan. Mix together pumpkin, milk, eggs, allspice and salt; pour into crust. Sprinkle reserved crumb mixture over top. Bake at 350 degrees for 55 minutes. Cool and serve with whipped topping. Serves 8 to 10.

Stack several homebaked cookies then wrap with ribbon or raffia...a tasty gift for a co-worker to enjoy as an after-lunch treat.

Vanilla-Dipped Gingersnaps

Krista Starnes
Beaufort, SC

This is a cookie recipe I make every Christmas for friends & family.
These are not only pretty, but they taste delicious!

2 c. sugar
1-1/2 c. oil
2 eggs
1/2 c. molasses
4 c. all-purpose flour
4 t. baking soda

1 T. ground ginger
2 t. cinnamon
1 t. salt
additional sugar for coating
2 12-oz. pkgs. vanilla chips
1/4 c. shortening

Combine sugar and oil in a mixing bowl; mix well. Add eggs, one at a time, beating well after each addition. Stir in molasses. Combine flour, baking soda, ginger, cinnamon and salt in a separate bowl; gradually blend into molasses mixture. Shape dough into 3/4-inch balls and roll in additional sugar; place 2 inches apart on ungreased baking sheets. Bake at 350 degrees for 10 to 12 minutes or until cookie springs back when lightly touched. Remove to wire racks to cool. Melt vanilla chips and shortening together in a small saucepan over low heat, stirring until smooth. Dip each cookie halfway into mixture; allow excess to drip off. Place cookies on wax paper to harden. Makes about 14 dozen.

Brush rosemary sprigs lightly with corn syrup then dust with sugar...pretty "evergreen" sprigs for a gingerbread house!

Ho-Ho-Holiday Goodies

Candy Cane Cocoa

Pat Ghann-Akers
Bayfield, CO

This will warm you head-to-toe on those snowy nights.

4 c. milk
3/4 c. sugar
1 t. peppermint extract
1-1/2 c. baking cocoa

1 pt. mint chocolate chip
  ice cream
chocolate syrup
8 candy canes

Combine milk, sugar, peppermint extract and cocoa in a large saucepan. Heat over medium heat until hot; do not boil. Divide evenly into 8 large mugs. Float a scoop of ice cream in each mug; drizzle with chocolate syrup and serve with a candy cane in each. Makes 8 servings.

Turn a plain white pillowcase into a whimsical snowman! Stitch some buttons, eyes, a nose and mouth on a pillowcase, and then stuff with polyester fiberfill. Secure with a length of ribbon at the top and tie on a scarf...a terrific way to wrap a gift too!

Raspberry Jam Cookies

Mary Patenaude
Griswold, CT

Let the little ones add the thumbprints…Grandma will love them!

2/3 c. sugar
1 c. butter, softened
1/2 t. almond extract

2 c. all-purpose flour
1/2 c. raspberry jam

Combine sugar, butter and almond extract in a mixing bowl. Beat with an electric mixer at medium speed until creamy. Add flour; beat on low until well mixed. Shape dough into one-inch balls; place 2 inches apart on ungreased baking sheets. Indent a thumbprint in the center of each cookie. Fill each with 1/4 teaspoon jam. Bake at 350 degrees for 14 to 18 minutes or until edges are lightly golden. Let stand on baking sheets for one minute, then remove to wire racks to cool. Drizzle glaze over cooled cookies. Makes 3-1/2 dozen.

Glaze:

1 c. powdered sugar
1-1/2 t. almond extract

2 to 3 t. water

Stir together powdered sugar and almond extract. Gradually stir in enough water to form a thin glaze.

Create a tasty advent tradition. Place 24 wrapped cookies inside a cookie jar. Each day, beginning December 1st, little ones can reach in and enjoy a treat. When all the treats are gone, Santa's on his way!

Ho-Ho-Holiday Goodies

Peanutty Cherry Squares

Susan Van Ormer
Madison, SD

A creamy cherry layer between chocolate and peanuts...yum!

2 c. sugar
2/3 c. evaporated milk
12 marshmallows
1/2 c. margarine
1/8 t. salt
6-oz. pkg. cherry chips

1 t. vanilla extract
12-oz. pkg. milk chocolate
   chips, melted
3/4 c. creamy peanut butter
1 c. chopped salted peanuts

Combine first 5 ingredients in a saucepan; bring to a boil and stir for 5 minutes. Add cherry chips and vanilla; remove from heat. Let stand, stirring occasionally. Stir together melted chocolate and peanut butter; mix in peanuts. Pour half the chocolate mixture into a 13"x9" baking pan. Pour cherry mix over chocolate layer, then top with remaining chocolate mixture. Refrigerate until firm; cut into squares. Makes 2 to 3 dozen.

If a traditional fruit-filled pie is on the dessert menu, add a new look to the traditional lattice-top. Twist strips of pastry and lay on top the fruit filling to form a pretty pinwheel-topped pie.

Holiday Honey Balls

Michele Walter
Lindenhurst, NY

For many years I enjoyed a place at my grandmother's side in her kitchen during the holidays. She would make this recipe and the warmth and wonderful smell of these treats made her kitchen feel like the best place in the world.

3 c. all-purpose flour, divided
1/2 c. sugar
2 t. baking powder
1/2 t. salt
4 eggs

1/4 c. butter, melted
oil for frying
1-1/2 c. honey
Optional: 3/4 c. pignoli nuts and
        colorful sprinkles

Mix together 2-1/2 cups flour, sugar, baking powder and salt; make a well in the middle and drop in eggs and butter. Mix well until dough leaves the sides of the bowl. Add remaining flour as needed. Turn dough out onto a floured surface and knead until dough is no longer sticky. Break off pieces of dough and roll into pencil-size ropes; slice into 1/2-inch pieces. Roll pieces into balls; set aside. Heat 2 inches oil in a skillet; fry balls until golden. Drain on paper towels. Heat honey in a saucepan over medium heat; bring to a boil and let boil for 3 to 4 minutes. Add fried balls, stirring gently until well coated. Remove balls from honey with a slotted spoon and place on a platter. Top with nuts and sprinkles if desired. Makes about 3 dozen.

For a special
one-of-a-kind gift,
fill vintage coffee
mugs with cookies
and candy…sure to
be a hit!

Ho-Ho-Holiday Goodies

Orange Slice Cake

Jennifer Allen
Tunas, MO

Mom's gift to Dad every Christmas.

1 c. butter
2 c. sugar
5 eggs
1 T. vanilla extract
4 c. all-purpose flour, divided
1/2 t. baking soda
1 t. salt

3/4 c. buttermilk
8-oz. pkg. dates, chopped
1 lb. orange slice candies,
  chopped
2 c. chopped pecans
4-oz. can flaked coconut

Cream together butter and sugar. Add eggs, one at a time, beating well after each addition. In a separate bowl, sift together 3-1/4 cups flour, baking soda and salt; add to creamed mixture alternating with buttermilk. In a separate bowl, toss remaining ingredients with remaining flour; fold into batter. Pour mixture into a greased and floured tube pan. Bake at 300 degrees for 2-1/2 hours. Cool slightly; invert onto platter and pour syrup over top. Serves 10 to 12.

Syrup:

1/4 c. orange juice
1/4 c. lemon juice

1/2 c. powdered sugar

Combine in a saucepan and bring to a boil, stirring until smooth.

It's that time of year when it's good to be fat & jolly!
-Unknown

Sour Cream-Chip Cookies

Bev Johnstone
Gooseberry Patch

Because these cookies are so soft and chewy, they're
my family's favorite treat any time of year!

1/2 c. margarine
1 c. brown sugar, packed
1/2 c. sugar
2 eggs
1 c. sour cream
1 t. vanilla extract

3 c. all-purpose flour
1/2 t. baking soda
6-oz. pkg. semi-sweet
　　chocolate chips
Optional: 1/2 c. chopped pecans

Blend together first 4 ingredients with an electric mixer until fluffy. Stir in sour cream and vanilla. Sift together flour and baking soda; add to creamed mixture. Stir in chocolate chips and pecans, if desired. Drop by rounded teaspoonfuls onto ungreased baking sheets. Bake at 375 degrees for 10 minutes. Makes 3 to 4 dozen.

Toasting nuts gives them a richer flavor...try it with the chopped pecans in Sour Cream Chip Cookies; it's simple! Spread nuts in a single layer in a shallow baking pan. Bake at 350 degrees for 5 to 10 minutes, stirring twice, until lightly golden.

Ho-Ho-Holiday Goodies

Buttercream Sandwich Cookies

Shelley Duffy
Winona, MN

These melt in your mouth.

1 c. butter
2 c. all-purpose flour

1/3 c. light cream
Garnish: colorful sugar

Cut butter into flour to cornmeal consistency; stir in cream. Roll dough out on a lightly floured surface to 1/8-inch thickness. Cut with a 2-inch round cookie cutter; place on ungreased baking sheets and sprinkle with sugar. Prick each cookie with a fork. Bake at 375 degrees for 8 to 10 minutes or until bottoms are golden. Remove to wire racks to cool. Spread a small amount of filling on the bottom side of half the cookies; top each with another cookie, sugared-side up, to make a sandwich. Makes 3 dozen.

Buttercream Filling:

1/4 c. butter
1 to 1-1/4 c. powdered sugar
3 T. milk

1 t. vanilla extract
Optional: food coloring

Beat butter until light and fluffy; gradually add one cup powdered sugar, beating well. Mix in milk and vanilla. Add more powdered sugar if necessary to reach desired spreading consistency. Stir in food coloring if desired.

When Santa's little helpers are lending a hand in the kitchen, remember to make plenty of each goodie to allow lots of taste tests!

Sweet Caramel-Chocolate Dip

Lisa Johnson
Hallsville, TX

Serve with your favorite dippers...strawberries, cherries, bananas, marshmallows and graham crackers taste great!

14-oz. pkg. caramels, unwrapped
5-oz. can evaporated milk

1/2 c. semi-sweet chocolate chips
1/2 t. vanilla extract

Place caramels in an ungreased 8"x8" baking pan. Stir in remaining ingredients. Bake at 350 degrees for 30 minutes. Stir until smooth. Makes 2 cups.

Creamy Peanut Butter Fudge

Pamela Howe
Kingfield, ME

I love snuggling under a blanket with my cat while watching old Christmas movies and nibbling on this fudge!

4 c. sugar
1/2 c. butter
1 c. milk

12-oz. jar creamy peanut butter
4 oz. marshmallow creme
2/3 c. all-purpose flour

Bring sugar, butter and milk to a boil in a saucepan; boil for 5 minutes and remove from heat. Stir in remaining ingredients; beat until smooth. Pour in a 13"x9" baking pan lined with wax paper and chill until firm. Cut into squares. Makes 4 to 5 dozen.

Chocolate Silk Pie

Jamie Moffatt
French Lick, IN

Cut generous slices of this pie...everyone will love it!

1 c. sugar
1/8 t. salt
1/2 c. baking cocoa
1/2 c. all-purpose flour
2 c. milk
3 egg yolks
4 T. butter

1 t. vanilla extract
9-inch graham cracker pie crust
8-oz. container frozen whipped
  topping, thawed
1/2 c. chocolate chips
Garnish: mint leaves

Combine sugar, salt, cocoa and flour in a saucepan over medium heat. Slowly pour in milk, stirring constantly. Pour in egg yolks; stir well for 5 to 6 minutes. Remove saucepan from heat; stir in butter and vanilla. Pour mixture into pie crust. Refrigerate for 8 hours. Top with whipped topping and chocolate chips. Garnish with fresh mint leaves. Serves 6 to 8.

Need a homemade treat in half the time?
Pick up peanut butter cookie dough at the grocery
store and wrap a tablespoon of dough around
bite-size candy bars. Bake at 350 degrees for 12 to
15 minutes...so yummy!

Christmas Rainbow Cake

Karen Whitby
Charlotte, VT

*For a holiday touch, roll out gumdrops and then cut to
resemble holly leaves and berries.*

18-1/2 oz. pkg. moist white
   cake mix
3-oz. pkg. raspberry gelatin mix
3-oz. pkg. lime gelatin mix

2 c. boiling water, divided
12-oz. container frozen whipped
   topping, thawed

Prepare cake mix according to package directions; pour batter into
2 greased 8" round baking pans. Bake as directed and allow to cool for
10 minutes; remove from pans and cool completely. Place cake layers,
top-sides up, back into cleaned cake pans. Prick each layer with a fork
every 1/2 inch. Pour one cup boiling water over raspberry gelatin in a
small bowl; stir until dissolved. Spoon raspberry mix over one layer.
Repeat with lime gelatin, pouring over the second layer. Refrigerate
cakes for 3 to 4 hours. Dip one cake pan into a pan of warm water to
loosen cake; invert onto a plate, removing pan. Spread one cup
whipped topping over layer. Remove second cake from pan like the
first, and invert on top of the first layer. Frost cake with remaining
topping. Serves 6 to 8.

A 2 or 3-tier pie stand is ideal for serving a variety
of cookies and candies. Set a plate on each tier and fill
with goodies galore!

Ho-Ho-Holiday Goodies

Bûche De Noël

Pamela Preston
Zanesville, OH

This traditional French cake resembles the Yule logs of long ago.

1/2 c. cake flour
1/4 c. baking cocoa
1 t. baking powder
1/4 t. salt
1/2 c. sugar
3 eggs, separated
1/4 c. milk

2 T. powdered sugar
2-3/4 c. whipping cream,
    divided
8 1-oz. sqs. semi-sweet baking
    chocolate, melted
1/4 c. butter, softened

Grease a jelly-roll pan and line with wax paper; grease paper. Set pan aside. Sift together flour, cocoa, baking powder and salt. Beat together sugar and egg yolks with an electric mixer on high speed until light and fluffy. At low speed, alternately beat milk and flour mixture into egg mixture. Using clean beaters, beat egg whites at high speed until stiff, but not dry, peaks form. Fold 1/3 beaten whites into batter. Fold in remaining whites. Spread batter in prepared pan; smooth top. Bake cake at 350 degrees until set, about 12 minutes. Dust a clean cloth with powdered sugar and turn cake out onto prepared cloth. Remove wax paper and trim cake edges. Starting with a short side, roll up cake, jelly-roll style. Transfer, seam-side down, to a wire rack to cool for 30 minutes. Unroll cake; remove cloth. Beat 3/4 cup whipping cream until soft peaks form; spread over cake to within one inch of edges. Re-roll cake; place, seam-side down, on a serving plate. Bring remaining cream, chocolate and butter to a boil in a saucepan over medium heat. Stir vigorously until blended. Remove from heat and let stand until set. Spread frosting over top and sides of cake. Serves 8 to 10.

Add edible poinsettia squares to dress up any cake or pie. Make strawberry wedges to form the flowers and tuck in a few mint leaves around each...charming!

Cream-Filled Pumpkin Roll

Susan Greeves
Frederick, MD

You can make this beautiful dessert...it's easier than you think!

1 c. sugar
3/4 c. all-purpose flour
1 t. baking powder
1 t. cinnamon

1/8 t. salt
3 eggs, beaten
2/3 c. canned pumpkin
3 T. powdered sugar, divided

Mix together first 5 ingredients; blend in eggs and pumpkin. Pour batter into a buttered jelly-roll pan lined with wax paper; spread evenly. Bake at 375 degrees for 15 minutes or until center tests done. Lay a kitchen towel down on a flat surface and sprinkle 2 tablespoons powdered sugar over top. Cut around sides of pan to loosen cake; invert onto sugared towel, wax paper-side up. Fold one side of towel over one long side of cake, then roll up jelly-roll style. Cool cake completely. Unroll cake and leave on towel; peel off wax paper. Spread filling evenly over cake. Use towel to help roll up cake and place seam side-down on a serving platter. Trim ends of cake and dust with remaining powdered sugar. Cover and refrigerate until serving. Serves 8 to 10.

Cream Cheese Filling:

8-oz. pkg. cream cheese, softened
1 c. powdered sugar
2 T. unsalted butter, softened

1 t. vanilla extract
Optional: 1/2 c. chopped walnuts

Combine cream cheese, sugar, butter and vanilla; blend well. Stir in walnuts, if desired.

For a frosty glow, wrap rice paper around the outside of a glass chimney before tucking the candle inside.

Ho-Ho-Holiday Goodies

Luscious Layered Brownies

Vickie

No need to frost...lay on a stencil or paper doily and dust with powdered sugar for a very pretty finishing touch.

3/4 c. all-purpose flour
3/4 c. baking cocoa
1/4 t. salt
1/2 c. butter, sliced
1/2 c. sugar
1/2 c. brown sugar, packed
3 eggs, divided

2 t. vanilla extract
1 c. chopped pecans
3/4 c. white chocolate chips
1/2 c. caramel ice cream topping
3/4 c. semi-sweet chocolate
  chips

Mix together flour, cocoa and salt in a bowl; set aside. In a separate bowl, blend together butter and sugars until creamy. Add 2 eggs, one at a time, beating well after each addition. Mix in vanilla. Gradually beat in flour mixture. Reserve 3/4 cup batter; spread remaining batter into a greased 8"x8" baking pan. Sprinkle pecans and white chocolate chips over batter. Drizzle caramel topping over top. Beat remaining egg into reserved batter until light in color; stir in chocolate chips. Spread evenly over caramel topping. Bake at 350 degrees for 30 to 35 minutes or until center tests done. Cool and cut into squares. Makes 12 to 16.

Cut brownies into bite-size squares and slip a party pick into each...ice skaters can glide by and get a treat without even removing a mitten!

Nana's Christmas Pudding

Annmarie Heavey
Bridgewater, MA

When I was young my grandmother used to make this every year…and only at Christmas. I used to believe that was the only time it could be made!

3-oz. pkg. lime gelatin mix
3-oz. pkg. cook & serve vanilla
  pudding

1/2 pt. whipping cream
29-oz. can fruit cocktail

Prepare gelatin according to package directions; pour into serving bowl and chill until semi-firm. Cook pudding according to package directions; cool. Whip cream and fold all the ingredients together in serving bowl, adding the undrained fruit cocktail. Chill until ready to serve. Makes 8 servings.

Baking goodies when time allows and then freezing them is a great time-saver as the holidays draw near. To keep frozen treats tasting fresh remember to wrap them in self-sealing freezer bags and follow these timelines: unfrosted cookies will keep fresh for 3 months, cheesecakes for one month, baked and unbaked fruit pies for 4 months.

Ho-Ho-Holiday Goodies

Red Velvet Cake

Stephani Hobert
Huber Heights, OH

This colorful cake is a terrific choice for a holiday dessert buffet.

1/2 c. shortening
1-1/2 c. sugar
2 eggs
2-oz. bottle red food coloring
2 t. baking cocoa
1 t. salt

2-1/2 c. all-purpose flour
1 t. vanilla extract
1 c. buttermilk
1 t. baking soda
1 t. vinegar

Cream together shortening, sugar and eggs. In a separate bowl, mix together food coloring and cocoa; add to creamed mixture. Add salt, flour, vanilla and buttermilk. Alternately add baking soda and vinegar until just blended. Pour batter into 2 greased and floured 8" round baking pans. Bake at 350 degrees for 30 minutes. Cool. Spread frosting on layers and stack to form a 2-layer cake. Serves 6 to 8.

Frosting:

3 T. all-purpose flour
1 c. milk
1 c. sugar

1 c. shortening
1 t. vanilla extract

Combine flour and milk in a saucepan; cook over medium heat until thick. Cool. Cream together sugar, shortening and vanilla until fluffy; add to flour mixture. Beat until light and fluffy.

Index

Index

Index

Salads

Sides

Gift Mixes

Crafts

We've cooked up a whole collection of Gooseberry Patch® books!

Have a taste for more? Call us toll-free at
1-800-854-6673

We'll send you our latest catalog filled with snowmen, Santas, ornaments, candles, cookie cutters, gourmet goodies, calendars, giftwrap, pottery, collectibles and MORE...including our best-selling cookbooks!

Phone us:
1·800·854·6673

Fax us:
1·740·363·7225

Visit our website:
www.gooseberrypatch.com

Send us your favorite recipe!

Include the memory that makes it special for you too! If we select your recipe for a brand new **Gooseberry Patch** cookbook, your name will appear right along with it...and you'll receive a FREE copy of the book! Mail to:

Vickie & Jo Ann
Gooseberry Patch, Dept. Book
600 London Road
Delaware, Ohio 43015

*Please include the number of servings and all other necessary information!

223

Rances ✦ TWINKLING LIGHTS ✦ FROSTY WINDOW PANES ✦ SNUGGLY QUILTS ✦ WARM MITTENS ✦ SLEIGHBELLS & MISTLETOE ✦ SNOW ANGELS ✦ FUZZY SWEATERS ✦ SPICY GINGERBREAD MEN ✦ HANDMADE ORNAMENTS ✦ FAMILY & FRIENDS ✦ SWEET REMEMB